THE MADMAN AND THE NUN

&

THE CRAZY LOCOMOTIVE

Three Plays

(including **THE WATER HEN**)

by Stanisław Ignacy Witkiewicz

Edited, Translated and with an Introduction
by Daniel Gerould
and
C.S. Durer

For

THEATRE BOOK PUBLISHERS
211 West 71 Street, New York, NY 10023

LIBRARY OF CONGRESS CATALOGING-IN-PUBLICATION DATA

Witkiewicz, Stanisław Ignacy, 1885-1939.
  [Plays. English. Selections.]
  Madman and the nun & The crazy locomotive: three plays, including The water hen / by Stanisław Ignacy Witkiewicz; edited, translated and with an introduction by Daniel Gerould and C.S. Durer; foreword by Jan Kott.
     p.   cm.
  Selected plays, translated from the Polish.
  ISBN 0-936839-83-X: $7.95
  1. Witkiewicz, Stanisław Ignacy, 1885-1939—Translations, English.
I. Title. II. Title: Madman and the nun and The crazy locomotive.
PG7158.W52A24 1988
891.8'527—dc19

                                                              88-7715
                                                              CIP

APPLAUSE THEATER BOOK PUBLISHERS
211 West 71st Street
New York, NY 10023
(212) 595-4735

First Applause Printing, 1989
Printed in the U.S.A.

THE MADMAN AND THE NUN

&

THE CRAZY LOCOMOTIVE

CONTENTS

Foreword

I MET Stanisław Ignacy Witkiewicz five or six years before the Second World War. I was then a student, and Witkiewicz sometimes dropped by as a guest to the seminars given by the Philosophy Department of Warsaw University. I knew his two novels and some of his plays that had been published in magazines or were circulating in manuscript copies. I saw many of his paintings; Witkacy (the name he created for himself from the first part of his last name and the last part of his middle name) was very popular as a painter. He was making portraits at a low price, and he often gave them away free of charge. Later on I met some of his personal friends, or rather his "ex-" friends; Witkacy called them his "ideological enemies." He had the practice of keeping a numbered list of his acquaintances, and whenever he lowered the position of one of them, he would inform him about it with an "official" letter. Once as an annual, or semestrial, assignment, I wrote about his theory of Pure Form. Later on he invited me to his house. He showed me his collection of canes of famous women, artists, and politicians. There was among them, if I remember correctly, the little cane of Marie Curie-Skłodowska and the umbrella of the great pianist Ignacy Paderewski who, after the restoration of Polish independence, became the prime minister of the first Polish government.

I was under the spell of Witkacy; however, I was more fascinated by his personality and himself than by his creative work. I knew that he was an extraordinary and splendid man, but at the same time I did not have the slightest doubt that his extraordinariness and splendor belonged to another epoch. To the future? No! To the past. Witkacy as a man, writer, and artist seemed to me like a dazzling relic from the beginning of the twentieth century who had strayed into contemporary times.

It would not be worth mentioning this opinion of a young student from thirty years ago were it not for the fact that it was currently shared both by young intellectuals and by mature writers. By definition a precursor is one who swerves away from his own times. As a precursor of the Theater of the Absurd, Witkacy was the most eminent playwright in Poland and one of the most interesting in Europe. But he was also—and this may be most astonishing—one of the most original precursors of what might be called the intellectual and artistic climate of the sixties, of its style of life and of thinking. And not only in Europe, but in America as well. Witkacy, who came too early, seemed

to his contemporaries to be a man who came too late. It would be
worth while to devote some attention to this very phenomenon of the
precursor who swerves away from his time or, to be more precise, to
the problem of the dialectic of anachronism and innovation.

Let us begin with the simplest question, with Witkacy's painting.
Witkiewicz had the rare gift, even among painters, of a rapid grasp of
resemblances. His portraits resembled their models, even those paintings—the most expensive according to his price list—which were made
under the influence of narcotics, and which were visionary and de-
formed. At that time the leading school of painters in Poland were
the postimpressionists, for the most part students of Bonnard. The
younger or more "modern" painters continued the experiments of the
constructivists and cubists; they rigorously practiced abstract painting.
Max Ernst and the surrealists were still at that time almost unknown in
Poland. Witkiewicz was somewhat slighted by painters; they considered his painting "literary," and this "literariness" was very badly
regarded by artists at that time. The postimpressionists and the post-
cubists as well were preoccupied with form, quality of color, and composition; they were not interested in qualities that were extrinsic to the
painting. According to them, Witkacy—the theoretician of Pure Form
—was painting old-fashioned, figurative pictures. For them even his
visions were illustrations.

I think that the painters were quite right. Today, from a greater
perspective in time, the connections that link Witkacy's painting with
the English pre-Raphaelite school and with the Viennese Secession are
obvious. The cold blue tones, the violet and rose colors in Witkacy's
pastels, his unreal, ghostly lighting derive from Arnold Böcklin's painting; his thin, vanishing, and undulating stroke, like the unfolding coils
of a snake, is more ornamental than pictorial and comes closest to the
style of Edward Burne-Jones. But what was generally considered in the
twenties and thirties to be passé became a live inspiration a quarter of ⹁
century later.

The Viennese Secession, anathemized as the epoch of the decline of
taste, has come back triumphantly into fashion with the revival of the
Art Nouveau influence in furniture and perhaps most of all in posters.
It has become a new tenet of style. Witkacy's portraits and composi-
tions often strikingly call to mind the psychedelic posters which have
become a new art form for collectors. Witkacy's faces, which emerge
from a colorful mist with their magnified eyes, their grimacing mouths,
and all their striking resemblance to their models, are first of all
psychological portraits. There is always tension and anxiety in them, a
kind of tragic absence; they are faces from a narcotic "trip."

Witkacy used the term Pure Form for the particular metaphysical quality in painting and poetry which cannot be analyzed into its primary elements; he called it "unity within diversity" or "the mystery of existence." It is not astonishing that this was not understood by painters; for them, form consisted in lighting on a surface and the composition of masses, and not in any "metaphysical qualities."

Witkacy was undoubtedly one of the precursors of the philosophy of "existence," but although he introduced symbols and quasi-mathematical formulas into his argumentation, his language recalled that of the nineteenth-century spiritualists rather than that of the twentieth century's precise and technical philosophizing. To the Marxists, to the phenomenologists, and most of all to the neopositivists, Witkacy's theories were "metaphysics"; they were an accumulation of "empty" propositions which did not permit verification, that is, they were neither true nor false, and did not observe the formal rules of the manipulation of propositions.

For philosophers, Witkacy was an interesting, sometimes fascinating amateur; for writers and men of the theater, he was a painter who, as an amateur, dabbled in literature and the theater. Today Witkacy is more and more often described as a "Renaissance man," as one of the most universal European minds. In his own time, despite the great spell and fascination which he exerted, he was considered a dilettante; he did not fit into the intellectual and artistic community, which was rigidly compartmentalized and highly specialized. Nobody scoffed at the pretensions of artists to superhumanity and independent morality with more force than Witkacy. But in life, especially for the benefit of his friends, Witkacy often very readily put on the mask of a demon. He proclaimed in his theory that modern art is more and more compelled toward perversion, which, translated into more normal language, meant the necessity of formal refinement and of shock-producing means of expression. In addition, he defended the right to perversion in life. This "demonism," which was so characteristic of many generations of the European bohemia, seemed, in the years between the two wars, frightfully old-fashioned.

As a young man, Witkacy walked through the streets of Zakopane in a harlequin's costume; he liked to disguise himself until the end of his life. He adored all forms of social and intellectual provocation; he treated life as a game and a play; certainly he had much in common with Oscar Wilde. But now, from the perspective of a greater distance of time, it becomes obvious that although he lived his life as a play, the genre of the play was tragedy.

Witkacy was, or acted (the adopted mask is also the face) the role of, an aristocrat of the spirit and the intellect, of a bohemian and, most rarely, of a dandy. All these personal patterns—of a liberated artist, of

an artist at odds with society, of an artist misunderstood by the philis-
tines—seemed in the interwar period extremely "nineteenth century."
In the period between the Spanish Civil War and the outbreak of the
Second World War, intellectuals began to be fascinated by political
movements and by the idea of "engagement." For all its naïveté, the
diagnosis by Julian Benda in his well-known book, *The Treason of the
Intellectuals*, was basically accurate. Of course the "engagement" was
understood by intellectuals in various ways. Some considered that the
function of a writer was that of agitator; some, of an ideologist; others
thought, finally, that the preparation of a revolution or a *coup d'état* is
the only important intellectual and moral experience of a twentieth-
century writer. The best examples of these attitudes were: the adher-
ence of the majority of the French surrealists to the Communist party,
the participation of André Malraux and many Anglo-Saxon writers in
the Spanish Civil War, Bertolt Brecht's political and didactic theater,
and, on the side of the "Establishment," Jean Giraudoux as minister and
Paul Claudel as the French ambassador in the United States. Just as
Witkacy did not fit into any of the professional compartments of
intellectual and artistic milieux that were becoming more and more
technical, so he did not fit into the division of the political left and
right. Nor did he have any liberal illusions. His basic nonconformism
resulted from various historical experiences and implied something
different. Once again, this particular nonconformity diverged from the
attitudes of his epoch. It occurred earlier, and it will occur later.
Witkacy's nonconformism was probably closest to that of Alexander
Blok, Leo Shestov, and a large part of the pre-Revolutionary Russian
intelligentsia. Today we can find a similar type of nonconformity and
rebellion against the establishment in the posture of Dylan Thomas,
John Arden, and Allen Ginsberg.

The main road of the Berkeley campus of the University of California ends at the intersection of two streets: Bancroft and Telegraph. On
this corner, a man with a hoarse voice and a middle-aged woman sing
psalms every day at about noon. Next to them barefoot girls and
long-haired, disheveled boys wearing strings of beads over colorful
shirts sell the *Berkeley Barb*. Two hundred feet toward the center of
the campus there is a square with a fountain between the Student
Union and the wide, amphitheatrical steps of the administration building; here stand the tables of the various student groups and organiza-
tions. And here you can buy a red booklet with Mao Tse-tung's
thoughts, sign a protest against the war in Vietnam, enroll in several
political parties or in the sexual freedom league. Psychedelic leaflets
with the same flowery, serpentine designs invite you to attend a Baptist

service, to join a nudist group, to take judo lessons, or to devote yourself to either Christian or Buddhist meditation. This little square on the Berkeley campus, where every day numerous scenes from Witkacy's plays are performed with few changes by young boys and girls who have never heard of their author, is one of the most sensitive barometers of the intellectual ferment of American youth. One can find similar squares, although perhaps less intense and colorful, on other American campuses also; and similar symptoms of ferment can be found in Swedish, English, and German universities. The atmosphere of the Berkeley campus resembles most, I think, the Russian universities before the 1905 revolution. Not only were the long locks of the boys and the short hair of the Russian female revolutionaries and suffragists similar, but also the furs worn over shirts, trousers tucked into high boots, or, in summer, sandals on bare feet—of course, taking off their student uniforms was a form of protest. But all these similarities are not the most important; each generation of artistic bohemia since Romanticism has performed some kind of a masquerade. The costume was like a uniform; it attested membership in a clan. The cape has been for a long time the uniform of a painter, just as the bowler has been the uniform of a London stockbroker.

More important than clothes and hair-do are the similarities of intellectual and ideological propositions. In the Russian universities at the beginning of our century, the followers of Tolstoy's belief in nonresistance to evil attempted to convince the apologists for terror that any form of violence is immoral. Socialists disputed with anarchists the need for the political activization of the masses and scoffed at individual herosim as if it were without political significance. The Russo-Japanese War laid bare the weakness of Tsarist Russia. The old religions were coming back, and new ones were born; the adherents to Buddhist Nirvana tried to convince the Old Believers of the new light coming from the East. At the universities the causes of free love and equality of sexual rights for women were advocated; hashish was smoked, ether was inhaled, and the first drug mystics appeared. Most of the time they drank, of course, vodka; but it was a Slavic way of drinking vodka: full of passionate discussions, of "stripping one's soul" and intimate confessions—drunken nights like trips down to the bottom.

At that time Witkacy was at the Academy of Fine Arts in Cracow. Cracow's bohemia was meager and provincial, but the Polish students who had gone to Russian universities violently radicalized somnolent Cracow and its artistic, "aesthetic" milieu. Witkiewicz saw the "naked soul" in its Russian version, a new Apocalypse and one of the ends of the world, only ten years later when he was a cadet in Pavlovski's regiment of the tsar's bodyguard and then the political commissar of a revolutionized division.

All historical analogies are true only up to a point, and are only one means of interpretation. History does not repeat itself, or repeats itself each time in a different way; and if outlived social forms, as Marx wrote, die twice, first as tragedy, then as farce, the grotesque is always both farce and tragedy, a third death of old forms.

It is easier, however, to understand Witkacy's swerving from his time and the contemporaneity of his theater—so striking today—if we compare even for a moment the ideological ferment of the sixties with the Russian universities at the beginning of the century, the similar revolt against the establishment by the children of the same establishment, the contempt of the intellectuals for professional politicians, and the basic nonconformism of the artistic milieux.

It may be that, in the United States, these similarities are especially emphatic, and Witkacy's plays have not only their Polish or European contemporaneity but also their very special American contemporaneity. I realized this while directing *The Madman and the Nun* at San Francisco State College in 1967. A few small changes in the references to books that had been read by the hero were sufficient to make him appear as an incarnation of an American beatnik shut up in an insane asylum after a "bad trip." He had been put there as a dangerous madman, but his madness was, in fact, simply protest, contempt and hatred for the society of satisfied and obedient men. The hero is a madman for the physicians; but truly mad are the physicians themselves, and the whole world is insane.

If we consider the Theater of the Absurd, the Theater of Cruelty, and the Theater of Happenings as the most significant theatrical phenomena of the fifties and sixties, it no longer seems difficult to draw their historical genealogy. But this is true only today, because ten years ago the history of twentieth-century European theater seemed quite different. It was Martin Esslin who first drew the outline of this genealogy.

The origins of this modern theater go back to the scandal at the opening night of Alfred Jarry's *Ubu the King* in Paris in 1896, to Frank Wedekind's grotesque and demoniac tragedies, and, later on, to August Strindberg's works, especially *A Dream Play* (1902) and *The Ghost Sonata* (1907).

The second stage of development comprises German Expressionist drama from Oscar Kokoschka, Yvan Goll, and Georg Kaiser to Brecht's early plays, the literary cabarets in Berlin and Munich, and the Dadaist Cabaret Voltaire in Zürich during the last years of the First

World War. The third, most important stage was Antonin Artaud's
Theater of Alfred Jarry (1926–28), and the theater of Witkiewicz,
who wrote almost all his plays between 1918 and 1925.

> LEON But let's not have any dramas à la Ibsen, with all that tragedy
> business about the various professions and the shortcomings of each.
> I'd rather have a cold-soup tragedy or a meat-with-all-the-juices-
> cooked-out-of-it tragedy à la Strindberg.
> MOTHER Nothing's sacred to you. You treat Ibsen and Strindberg just
> the same way you treat me. Is there any greater work of genius in the
> whole world than Strindberg's *The Ghost Sonata?*
>
> [*The Mother*, Act I]

One of the first plays performed in Artaud's theater was Strindberg's
A Dream Play. But even a very superficial analysis of Witkacy's *The
Mother* and *The Water Hen* reveals that their author continues the
destruction of naturalistic theater exactly from the point where Strindberg stopped. The same was true for Artaud. In both Artaud's and
Witkiewicz' plays, even before the body of a character who has died
has time to cool down, he stands up and walks.

There is a long theatrical history behind characters who, after their
death, come back on stage in order to haunt living people or to give
them moral lessons; this should become the subject of a separate book.
The dead come back on stage both in Shakespeare and in Elizabethan
drama, both in Romantic and in modern drama. The dead come back
either as ghosts or as hallucinations. The ghost is a metaphysical premise; the hallucination is a psychological situation. But both imply, in the
properly theatrical sense, that the ghost or hallucination can be seen
only by some of the characters on the stage, that it behaves in a
different way from the "living" characters, it speaks differently, it
moves differently, it often wears the costume of a ghost or hallucination, and if it does not have a costume, then it still must have some
special traits or marks. The theatrical tradition of the behavior of
ghosts was probably undermined for the first time by Strindberg. In
The Ghost Sonata the dead Consul, wrapped in a winding sheet, comes
out of the door of the house where he died the day before to look at
the flag flying at half mast and to count the poor who came to his
funeral. Only the Student, however, sees him. A young girl, whom
many years ago Company Director Hummel had seduced and drowned,
appears as a Milkmaid in the first scene; she does not speak, but she
behaves normally. She even gives a cup of water to the Student. At the
beginning only he sees her. The Milkmaid will, however, appear in the
same act for a second time; she will raise her arms like one who is
drowning and gaze fixedly at her murderer. The metaphysical premise

of these apparitions is ambiguous in Strindberg's play; maybe they are ghosts, maybe only hallucinations. From the theatrical point of view, however, they no longer have otherworldly attributes.

But it is only in the plays with "corpses" of Artaud and Witkiewicz that the dead characters come back on stage in an ordinary manner. In *The Water Hen* the heroine who is shot in the first act comes back in the second act as if nothing had happened. In the third act, she is shot once again, but this time definitively. In *The Mother*, old Mrs. Eely dies in the second act. In the third act she lies in state, but this does not hinder her from appearing simultaneously as a person thirty years younger and, moreover, pregnant, expecting the birth of the hero of the play. The "first" Mother who is lying in state turns out to be a dummy. In *The Madman and the Nun* the corpse of a murdered psychiatrist, which has been removed by hospital attendants, comes back after a while, smiling, with the murderer who had hanged himself in the previous scene. His corpse is still on stage and is, of course, a dummy. The same thing happens in Artaud's pantomime *The Philosopher's Stone*, where Harlequin, who has been cut in pieces a moment ago by the jealous Doctor, jumps up from the operating table and immediately has sexual intercourse with the Doctor's wife, Isabella. After a while a baby is shaken out from her skirt who resembles the doctor as closely as two peas in a pod. The Harlequin who was tortured on the operating table was, of course, a dummy. The resemblance between Artaud's and Witkiewicz' plays using corpses is all the more surprising since Artaud could in no way have known Witkacy's plays. This theatricalization of corpses is very important in the history of the contemporary, avant-garde theater; the centuries-old convention of portraying the return of the dead in European theater was completely broken.

In the Chinese theater, when the hero dies or is killed he drops and lies flat for a moment and then runs off the stage. He has died, thus he has ceased to exist, and consequently he cannot be present on the stage. For a European spectator this convention seems surprising at first, yet it does not lack theatrical logic. The actor acts the role of a character, but it is impossible to act the role of a corpse; at most it is possible to simulate it. But to simulate a corpse means, in theatrical language, to pass from the technical means of "acting" to the technical means of "pantomime." The only difference is that it is a pantomime with no gestures. After the performance and after the curtain calls, the corpses get up to bow before the audience; they might just as well have got up earlier.

In the Japanese Nō theater, also, the dead—who return to haunt those who are alive, or to revenge themselves, or to reward their

benefactors—do not follow the theatrical premise of a European
"ghost." They behave, as far as I know, like characters who are alive,
that is to say, according to the same theatrical convention of gestures
and without any change in make-up. In the Bali theater, ghosts and
demons are represented as huge and lurid puppets. Artaud wrote about
the Bali theater:

> There is in the truly terrifying look of their devil (probably Tibetan)
> a striking similarity to the look of a certain puppet in our own remem-
> brance, a puppet with swollen hands of white gelatine and nails of green
> foliage, which was the most beautiful ornament of one of the first plays
> performed by Alfred Jarry's theater.[1]

The theater in which the dead are puppets and in which the dead get
up and walk—the theater which breaks away from the convention of
European drama—originated in the fascination with the Oriental theater. Artaud experienced this fascination when he saw the Bali theater
during the colonial exposition in Paris. The Chinese opera and the
Japanese Nō theater fascinated Brecht, too. From the Oriental theater
he adopted the ways in which the mask was used, symbolical make-up,
and pantomime elements in acting as the basic means of theatricalization and of producing the effect of alienation.
We do not know anything about Witkacy's theatrical experiences
during the time when he traveled in Australia and Malaysia. It seems
unlikely, however, that when he accompanied Malinowski to New
Guinea in 1914 and passed through India, Ceylon, and the Malayan
archipelago, Witkacy did not take an interest in or see any Oriental
theater. For a foreigner who does not know the language this is
primarily a visual theater, a theater of gesture, costume, and movement,
a true theater of Pure Form. But this theater of Pure Form is at the
same time a ritual and a liturgy. Antonin Artaud understood this
theater in exactly the same fashion, as pure spectacle and as ritual, and
he opposed it to the deadness of European theater. In the chapter
"Metaphysics and the *Mise en Scène*" from *The Theater and Its
Double*, he wrote: "In any case, and I hasten to say it at once, a theater
which subordinates the *mise en scène* and production, i.e., everything
in itself that is specifically theatrical, to the text, is a theater of idiots,
madmen, inverts, grammarians, grocers, antipoets and positivists, i.e.,
Occidentals." [2] In its formulation, even in its style, choice of words, and
terms this statement surprisingly resembles Witkacy's theories about
the theater of Pure Form.

[1] Antonin Artaud, *The Theater and Its Double*, trans. M. C. Richards (New
York: Grove Press, 1958), p. 56.
[2] *Ibid.*, p. 41.

"The last part of the spectacle," wrote Artaud about the Bali theater, "is—in contrast to all the dirt, brutality, and infamy chewed up by our European stages—a delightful anachronism. And I do not know what other theater would dare to pin down in this way as if true to nature the throes of a soul at the mercy of phantasms from the Beyond." [3]

These "throes of a soul at the mercy of phantasms from the Beyond" are like expressions Witkacy might have used, and they could characterize his painting and his theater. Witkacy's Theater of Pure Form and Antonin Artaud's Theater of Cruelty were to serve as the last places where metaphysical experiences which had been banished from philosophy and had become dead in religion could be expressed. Artaud wrote: "In our present state of degeneration it is through the skin that metaphysics must be made to re-enter our minds." But Witkacy would have said: only through the perversion of form.

It may be most significant that in both Witkiewicz and Artaud we find the same infernal fusion, the same explosive combination of two notions, or rather of two visions, of the theater. One of them is the theater of ritual and liturgy, the theater of metaphysical transports, the theater in which—as Witkacy thought—the "Mystery of Existence" will shake even the unbelievers. Or, as Artaud wrote, which "will restore to all of us the natural and magic equivalent of the dogmas in which we no longer believe." The other is the theater of violent physical action, the theater in which gestures, words, movements, and objects are not only a system of signs, but have their own pure theatrical value, just like a hieroglyph or Chinese ideogram which not only has a meaning but is an image as well.

In fact, these are two entirely different notions of theater, although both in Artaud and in Witkiewicz they are tightly interlaced like two fibers in one cord. From the perspective of another twenty-five years, it becomes clear that one of these visions of theater was an illusion. The magic counterpart of dogmas does not exist once you cease to believe in them. Ritual and liturgy in theater are either provocation or profanation of ritual and liturgy. This very profanation of ritual we can find in the theater of Genet, who is the only one to draw all of the consequences from Artaud's Theater of Cruelty.

In one of his rare moments of lucidity Artaud, however, was conscious of his illusion. In 1927 he wrote: "It is certain that if I had created a theater, what I would have done would have had as little relation to that which we are in the habit of calling 'theater,' as the representation of some obscenity resembles an ancient religious mystery." [4]

[3] *Ibid.*, p. 64.
[4] Antonin Artaud, *Oeuvres complètes* (Paris: Gallimard, 1961), II, 26.

In the real theater created by Witkiewicz, there are no metaphysical transports, nor is there any mystery of existence. And perhaps that is the reason why this theater became understood so late. Witkiewicz' theater is sometimes bitter, but always scoffing. The unquestionable greatness of this theater consists in its historical perspective, in the perception of the end of contemporary civilization which was fatally threatened both by the egalitarian revolution coming from the East and by Western mechanization. This mechanization not only produces a society of automatons, but also impels the automatons to direct even those who had invented them. Witkacy's catastrophism only apparently belongs to the nineteenth century. In fact, it was the perspicacious and appalling vision of an inevitable clash between the civilization of computers and the levelers' revolution. For Witkacy the nineteenth century ended once and for all in 1917. In this perspective, all that followed was grim and grotesque.

> EVADER Have you gone out of your mind? To play cards at such a critical time?
> FATHER At our age it's the only way of whiling away the time during a social upheaval. What else could we do? Whist or auction bridge? "That is the question." . . .
> TYPOWICZ One club.
> EVADER Two clubs.
> FATHER (*sitting down*) Two diamonds. (*A red glare floods the stage, and the monstrous boom of a grenade exploding nearby can be heard.*) Banging away in fine style. Your bid, Mr. Specter.
> SPECTER (*in a quivering, somewhat plaintive voice*) Two hearts. The world is collapsing. (*Fainter red flashes of lighting, and immediately afterward two shells exploding a little farther off*)
> TYPOWICZ Pass.
>
> [*The Water Hen*, Act III]

Until the outbreak of the Second World War, Witkacy was understood only by a few—maybe, because we were all still *before*, while he was already *after*.

JAN KOTT
Translated by Bogdana Carpenter

Introduction

PROLOGUE: WITKIEWICZ AND
THE AVANT-GARDE

THE DISCOVERY of an unknown dramatist of major stature is an exciting process, particularly when it comes thirty years after his death and when the reasons for both his initial obscurity and his subsequent fame are curiously intertwined with the history of European drama and civilization in the twentieth century. In the case of Stanisław Ignacy Witkiewicz (1885–1939), there are reasons for unusual excitement that go beyond his importance to the theater.

Witkiewicz is one of the most amazing artistic geniuses and personalities of the modern period. His range and productivity are incredible; playwriting was only one of the many artistic careers in which he excelled. Painter, playwright, critic, aesthetician, novelist, philosopher, and authority on drugs—Witkiewicz was a Renaissance man of the avant-garde who threw himself into art and life with a flamboyance and a fury unmatched except perhaps by Strindberg. His personal drama was as bizarre and colorful as any of his portraits or plays. His fantastic life and tragic death make him an almost mythical prototype of the artist in the twentieth century, the hero of one of his own dramas.

His creative versatility is a main source of his theater's originality and vitality. Witkiewicz was a superb painter, and his theater is strongly oriented toward painting, a fact which liberates it from the purely literary and gives it tremendous visual vividness and immediacy. His plays are composed as pictures, by colors, shapes, and lines. Witkiewicz was able to bring the experimental daring of modern painting to the theater and break through the purely imitative surface of drama —one of the major aims of the avant-garde in European theater. His many-sided genius and wide-ranging curiosity enabled him to explode the normal boundaries of the theater and bring the drama into line with the other arts and intellectual developments of the modern age.

Witkiewicz is unique in his ability to combine successfully three aspects of twentieth-century avant-garde drama which are rarely found together: fantasy, dreams, and a sense of the mystery of existence; penetrating social and political vision about the workings of history; and, finally, a mocking, irreverent humor and grotesque style built on parody and irony. In other words, Witkiewicz treats revolution, political and scientific totalitarianism, and the collapse of mechanized Western civilization with the poetic atmosphere of Cocteau's *Orpheus* and the breakneck comic verve of the Keystone Cops. Witkiewicz' theater goes far beyond categories such as expressionism and surrealism; his great strength as a playwright lies in his synthesis of different kinds of experience, different genres, and different styles.

To portray an international world of insanity where duchesses and policemen, gangsters and surrealist painters, psychiatrists and locomotive engineers wander in and out, kill one another, and carry on philosophical conversations at the same time, Witkiewicz developed a dramatic technique equally mad and free, full of sudden discontinuity, jerky motions, anticlimaxes, nonsequiturs, chases, free-for-alls, and rapidly accelerated tempos, as in a silent film.

Witkiewicz is a thoroughly original and underivative playwright. His "comedies with corpses," as he called them, present fantastically ludicrous visions of the violent self-destruction of mechanized Western civilization. Now Witkiewicz takes his place along with Strindberg, Alfred Jarry, and Artaud as one of the most original and powerful creative forces in the modern avant-garde theater, although his life ended in violent self-destruction and seeming total defeat. His triumph over oblivion has only been posthumous. Witkiewicz fought an endless battle with chaos, desperately trying to create something out of nothingness before it overpowered him. He lost—at least at first, in one dimension.

CREATION AND REVOLUTION

Stanisław Ignacy Witkiewicz was born in Warsaw on February 24, 1885. He started life as a Russian subject, since at that time Poland did not exist as an independent country, and Warsaw belonged to the tsar. Fifty-four years later, on September 18, 1939, Witkiewicz committed suicide as the new Polish state, a creation of Woodrow Wilson and the Treaty of Versailles, collapsed in defeat after only twenty years of life, attacked from the West by the Germans and from the East by the Russians. Within this period Witkiewicz led a life of the most frenzied artistic activity, trying to create against the chaos without and within that menaced him.

WITKIEWICZ, FATHER AND SON

His birthright was that of an artist. Helena Modjeska, the famous Polish actress who made her later career in America, was his god-

mother. His mother, Maria Pietrzkiewicz, was a music teacher, and his
father, Stanisław Witkiewicz, a famous and influential painter, architect, and art critic—an aggressive exponent of realistic technique, celebrated for his dictum that it was better to paint a head of cabbage
accurately than the head of Christ badly, no matter how devoutly. As a
theorist, the elder Witkiewicz was opposed to patriotic historical subjects and helped to dispel hazy romantic notions about the nature of
painting by his insistence on disregarding all that was extraneous to the
work of art.

Disillusioned with the results of industrialism and in reaction against
the positivists and positivism, the playwright's father advocated a return to the people and their culture and art. He was one of those
responsible for discovering the beauty of the Tatra mountains south
of Cracow and making them popular as scenic attractions. As an enthu-
siast for folklore, the elder Witkiewicz admired the picturesque qualities of the native peasant arts and crafts of the mountain region and
introduced a new house design based on the highlanders' log cabins,
called the Zakopane style of architecture after his favorite retreat in the
Tatras which has since become an internationally known tourist resort.
He found further outlet for his energies in mountain climbing, a sport
which he popularized in Poland.

Stanisław Ignacy Witkiewicz was an only son, and the relationship
between father and son was a close and friendly one. The father took
great interest in his son's talents and actively promoted his career in the
fine arts. For his part, young Witkiewicz always maintained intimate
ties with his father. After Witkiewicz, senior, was forced to leave
Poland and settle in Lovranno, Italy, in 1908 because of a tubercular
condition, his son came to visit him frequently until his death in 1915.

However, the lasting effect of such a dominating, successful father
on his less pragmatic son appears to have been something other than
their externally harmonious relations would indicate. Their interests
and attitudes to the world were diametrically opposed. The son was
addicted to other ways of seeing and other forms of exercise than his
father; he could not take things for what they are with his father's
brisk, clear-sighted vision—he looked within and beyond. He could not
abide the regional, the national, the exclusively Polish, and wanted to
get out and see the world. He reacted against the peasant art and
highlanders dear to his father's heart and regarded folklore with suspicion as a fraud devised by intellectual artists. In almost all his plays up
to *The Shoemakers* in 1934, there is more of the atmosphere of tropical
islands and the jungle than of the Tatra mountains.

To the end of his life, Stanisław Ignacy Witkiewicz remained the
son of a more famous father, both in his own eyes and in the eyes of

society. Early in life, he created the name Witkacy to distinguish himself from his father; he painfully felt the necessity to be great in his own right and the need to create a life and art of his own. He adored his mother and may have resented his father's treatment of her.[1] The family plays like *The Water Hen* and *The Mother* reflect these complexities and suggest that when Witkacy wrote, he tapped his deepest feelings about his father.

In 1890, when Witkacy was five years old, the family settled in Zakopane permanently for the sake of the elder Witkiewicz' health. Until the end of his life, Witkacy considered the small mountain retreat his home, the place to which ultimately he returned after his many travels. He remained the *enfant terrible* of Zakopane for the rest of his life, terrifying tourists with his striking appearance and his eccentric behavior.

Since in these early days there was no school in Zakopane, Witkacy was educated privately at home by a whole circle of tutors, usually friends of his father from the artistic and literary community. He was exposed to everything and allowed to pursue all that interested him. He never did receive methodical schooling or acquire academic discipline; he was self-taught as writer, painter, and philosopher, more an uncontrolled force of nature than a product of technical training. His lack of formal education simply served to heighten his vast intellectual curiosity and to increase his hunger for things of the mind. Insatiability was to become one of the key concepts in his philosophy of art and of life. As a child he was insatiable in his pursuit of knowledge in all fields.

His father's library and studio, his mother's piano and musical scores, and the circle of family friends, were his true education. As the only son of culturally eminent parents, Witkacy was brought up almost exclusively in the company of adults, for the most part artists and intellectuals. From an early age he listened to their talk and participated in it himself. He was raised in an atmosphere where he was special, where his talents could develop freely, where he could become an artist. His friends and contemporaries made up a remarkable group of the best talents of the time, many of whom were soon to gain fame far eclipsing his: the composer Karol Szymanowski, the pianist Artur Rubinstein, the anthropologist Bronislaw Malinowski, and the painter and philosopher Leon Chwistek.

Young Witkacy was a prodigious reader; as a child, he was allowed to read whatever he wanted, encouraged and helped by his father. He was first exposed to Shakespeare at a time when his father was working on an essay on *Hamlet;* the impact on his young imagination was

[1] Zbigniew A. Grabowski, "S. I. Witkiewicz: A Polish Prophet of Doom," *The Polish Review*, XII, No. 1 (Winter, 1967), 43.

obviously strong—his plays are full of Shakespearean quotations, references, parodies, and parallels, ranging from the appearance of Richard
III as a major character in *The New Deliverance* to the description of
Jeanne Cackleson, the railway guard's wife in *The Crazy Locomotive*,
"dressed all in white, decked out in flowers like Ophelia."

His childhood interests were not confined to the arts; he was a
voracious reader of scientific works as well. Once one of his aunts
stopped at Cracow, on her way to Zakopane, to buy the young Witkacy a present. She had decided to give her precocious nephew a
popular book on the natural sciences, but the owner of the bookstore
told her that she had better buy a specialized, scholarly study instead,
since Staś had already consumed all the elementary works. His plays
reflect his interest in science, especially the revolutionary discoveries of
modern mathematics and physics which have changed our ways of
seeing and understanding the world. Occasionally, as in *Tumor Brainard* (1921), instead of an artist, a mathematician as original as Einstein
becomes the defiant hero-genius at odds with society.

Another type of reading furthered young Witkacy's imaginative
journeys out of the world around him into other possible worlds of
adventure and daring. From the number of references in his works, it
would appear that *Treasure Island* and *Robinson Crusoe* were two of
his favorite books. A childhood fascination with pirates, a mysterious
island, and its dangerous games carries over into Witkacy's creative life
as a playwright and becomes a model for his view of society. He retains
his child's sense of fantasy and wonder about the strange and sinister
operations of the international world of crime and debauchery which
he invents as his Europe.

Robinson Crusoe offers Witkacy another key image: man alone on
his desert island, confronted with himself and a hostile outside world
—the terrifying adventure of being alive. Speaking of their engine-island, the engineer in *The Crazy Locomotive* tells his fireman: "We're
on our desert island again: Robinson Crusoe and his man Friday. We're
playing the Robinson game the way we did when we were children."
H. G. Wells and Jules Verne provided another kind of travel, into the
world of the future and of scientific technology which was to obsess
Witkacy and become one of the major themes in his drama and fiction.[2]
From childhood on he was in search of other worlds and other islands.

Art was his principal means, and Witkacy began to engage in artistic
creation very early. He started to paint under his father's tutelage, and
by the time he was eight he had already written many plays, of
which five very short examples survive. Witkacy's juvenile dramas

[2] Czeslaw Milosz, "S. I. Witkiewicz, a Polish Writer for Today," *Tri-Quar-
terly*, No. 9 (Spring, 1967), p. 150.

could be called a child's theater of the absurd. They reveal a number of traits characteristic of his mature dramaturgy: bizarre titles, subtitles, and names of characters; wildly accelerated action; fantasy and the grotesque; ludicrous dialogue; and concern with philosophical issues. In *Comic Scenes from Family Life*, an ironic picture of the Witkiewicz home life, puppetlike characters speak in clichés comparable to the language in the first draft of Ionesco's *The Bald Soprano*.[3] Scene 1 opens on the porch as Mrs. Dungly enters:

MAMA Good morning.
MR. DUNGLY Quite a storm we're having!
MAMA Yes, indeed! (*Enter Papa*)
PAPA Good morning.
MRS. DUNGLY Good morning. Well, I really must be going now.
PAPA Couldn't I lend you an umbrella? (*Mama and Papa go to get the umbrella.*)
MRS. DUNGLY Well, yes, thank you.
MAMA I'll get it for you.
PAPA It is raining. (*Exit Mrs. Dungly. Thunder and lightning*)[4]

In *Menagerie, or the Elephant's Prank*, the elephant misbehaves and attempts to take advantage of the lion, ape, and wolf, but is punished at the end and weeps penitently. *Cockroaches* is a play of terror tracing the reactions of the characters to the impending invasion of the castle by a swarm of cockroaches. *Princess Magdalena and the Overinsistent Prince* can be seen as a further, oblique comment on Witkacy's relations to his parents. It is a drama of thwarted love due to the opposition of the lovers' parents. King Wistilius' son commits suicide in despair, followed shortly by his father who has caused all the trouble. The play is an instant *Romeo and Juliet* in which everything happens with great rapidity. The son quotes Juliet's words, "O happy dagger! / This is thy sheath; there rust, and let me die," as he kills himself, in a combination of parody and unwitting prophecy.

Witkacy's first and last official sign of systematic study was the high-school diploma he was awarded in Cracow in 1903 on the basis of special examinations for nonattending students. Following his father's wish to make him a painter, Witkacy studied in a desultory fashion from 1904 to 1905 at the Cracow Academy of Fine Arts, where he was an unreceptive pupil. In his own painting and in his own theories, he rejected his father's ideal of fidelity to physical reality in favor of extreme distortion and inner truth. He preferred to paint fantastic por-

---

[3] Anna Micińska, "S. I. Witkiewicz, Iuvenilia," *Dialog*, No. 8 (August, 1965), p. 16.
[4] S. I. Witkiewicz, "Komedie z życia rodzinnego" ("Comic Scenes from Family Life"), *Dialog*, No. 8 (August, 1965), pp. 17–18.

traits rather than submit to the academy's discipline and stress on diligent copying. Whereas Witkiewicz the father battled against romanticism in the name of truth, the son declared war on realism and naturalism and all that is rational, symmetrical, and predictable.

From this point on Witkacy began a career of frenzied artistic activity—insatiable pursuit of form, as he called his never-ending search for the essence and the absolute. He soon abandoned landscape painting, which was his father's preferred genre; the son felt that competition with nature was both naïve and impossible as an artistic goal. Undoubtedly competition with his father seemed equally futile. In his portraits Witkacy attempted to portray his subject's inner self and penetrate into the subconscious. His art is a revelation of what lies beneath the surface of appearance and convention. In both painting and theater, Witkacy takes joy in ripping off masks; startling disclosure of hidden identity is one of his favorite dramatic techniques. "And now let's take off our masks" becomes the cry aboard *The Crazy Locomotive;* the engineer turns out to be Prince Tréfaldi, king of murderers, and his fireman, Travaillac, "sought in vain by the police all over the world."

Witkacy was a strikingly handsome man: tall, lean, with penetrating eyes and an intense, haunted look. Volatile and moody by nature, he swung between ecstasy and despair; he loved extremes and wanted all or nothing. An eccentric and a dandy, colorful, unpredictable, impossible to get along with, Witkacy was an individualist of gigantic proportions, an anarchist, a child in an alien world. Women adored him. "He was beautiful like an Archangel with those gray-green eyes of his. When he entered a cafe, my knees shook. And I guess all the women felt the same." These were the impressions of someone who knew him in Zakopane before the First World War.[5]

In his many self-portraits painted in a variety of different styles, the artist presents himself as demonic or demented. In a characteristic Mephistophelean pose, sharp, vicious lines create devilish brows, pointed ears, and a lean, fierce face. The eyes are almost squinting; a sinister hand with long, bony fingers dominates the foreground. In other, later self-portraits, Witkacy takes off this mask and reveals the anguish beneath. A shattered expression, crushed eyes, and terrible suffering emerge from a few rapidly drawn lines.

JOURNEYS TO OTHER WORLDS

Most important for Witkacy's development as an artist and philosopher were his travels outside of Poland—to the art museums of West-

[5] Czeslaw Milosz, "S. I. Witkiewicz, a Polish Writer for Today," p. 144.

ern Europe, to the South Sea Islands, and to Saint Petersburg at the time of the Revolution. The imaginary adventures of his childhood became real journeys of discovery.

Galleries

Witkacy's travels first opened his eyes to new ways of seeing and experiencing life and gave him the tools for portraying this vision. Not the Tatra mountains or the Cracow Academy of Fine Arts, but galleries in Paris were his inspiration both as a painter and as a playwright. In frequent trips to France, Germany, and Italy in the period before the First World War, Witkacy discovered the revolutionary movements in modern art that were rejecting naturalism and impressionism for abstraction. He visited the Gauguin exhibition in Vienna in 1907, seeing firsthand the works of an artist whose interest in the South Sea Islands anticipates Witkacy's own fascination with the primitive and exotic and whose rejection of Western civilization and its naturalistic tradition was congenial to his own point of view.

In Paris in the period from 1905 to 1913, Witkacy was exposed to the Fauves, the Futurists, and early cubism. His enthusiasm for the Fauves and for early Picasso is reflected in *They* (1920), one of his many plays devoted to art. The distortion, flat patterns, and violent colors of the Fauves indicate the direction that Witkacy himself was to take in his mature work both in painting and in the drama. His theater grows directly out of what he saw in the galleries in Paris; the inspiration of his dramas is pictorial, not literary. Because he was the dramatist as painter, he succeeded at a very early date in creating a nonrealistic dramaturgy based on a full-fledged and coherent nonrepresentational theory of the drama. Witkacy's work as a playwright springs directly from his experience of discovering Gauguin, Matisse, Derain, Picasso, and the other revolutionary masters of modern art, and from his own work as a painter and aesthetician.

Australia

Before becoming established as a painter in the period between the two world wars, Witkacy undertook two more trips that had far-reaching influence on his development as an artist and as a thinker. His next journey was to the South Seas with Bronislaw Malinowski, his childhood friend from Cracow who at the age of thirty was beginning his illustrious career as an anthropologist which would ultimately bring him to the United States in 1938 and a position at Yale University where he is buried. In the spring of 1914, the British Association for the Advancement of Science sent Malinowski to Australia and then to Papua (New Guinea) to work among the Mailu people, as a guest at the expense of the Australian government. Witkacy accompanied his friend in the capacity of photographer and draftsman.

The trip had been suggested and arranged by Witkacy's mother as a voyage of convalescence and recuperation from the tragic experiences of the preceding year. In 1913 his fiancée committed suicide, and he came down with typhoid. The expedition, which went via India, Ceylon, and the Malayan archipelago, was not always restful. There were endless quarrels and misunderstandings between Witkacy and Malinowski, neither of whom was willing to compromise or adapt to the other's stubbornness. By the outbreak of the war, the two friends had finally broken with one another for good, and Malinowski later recorded his anger and resentment in his diary:

> The Staś problem torments me. In fact his conduct towards me was impossible. . . . His complaints were unjustified, and the way he expresses himself precludes any possibility of reconciliation. *Finis amicitiae*. Zakopane without Staś! Nietzsche breaking with Wagner. I respect his art and admire his intelligence and worship his individuality, but I cannot stand his character.[6]

Their disagreements were often comic, the petty bickering of geniuses. One of these squabbles took a bizarre turn and had unforeseen complications as grotesque as in a Witkacy play and a surprising comic denouement like one of his own *coups de théâtre*. During a journey through the wilds of Australia, they came unexpectedly to the shores of a lake that cut off their projected route. They would have to skirt the lake in order to resume their cross-country travels, but, faced with the decision of whether to go to the right or the left, they simply could not agree. After a heated argument, they stubbornly insisted on their original positions and decided to split up temporarily, go their separate ways, and meet on the other side of the lake.

Malinowski was delayed in reaching the meeting place and therefore grew alarmed when he got there and found no trace of Witkacy. The anthropologist searched the surrounding bush, where he came upon a group of excited natives chanting and shouting. Malinowski's fears increased when he drew nearer and saw that the aborigines had a white man tied between two poles, stark naked, and that they were holding him high up over a small bonfire. When he recognized his friend Witkacy as the victim about to be roasted, Malinowski reached for his gun, but the next moment Witkacy yelled to him that the natives were helping him. On the trip around the lake, Witkacy had become cov-

[6] Bronislaw Malinowski, *A Diary in the Strict Sense of the Term* (New York: Harcourt, Brace & World, 1967), p. 34.

ered with ticks, and the natives with whom he quickly made friends were giving him the traditional heat treatment to get rid of ticks.

In such ways Witkacy acquired a taste for the exotic which is reflected in the descriptions of jungles and tropical scenery that occur in many of his plays and that he actually utilizes as the setting for several of his works. *Mister Price, or Tropical Madness* (1920) takes place in Rangoon where a heat wave drives the Europeans out of their minds, and *Metaphysics of a Two-headed Calf*, "A Tropical-Australian Play in Three Acts" (1921), has as its setting the royal governor's mansion in British New Guinea. The virility of the primitive races is contrasted with the decadence and intellectual dishonesty of the white Europeans. Although Witkacy always considered himself one of the last of an effete dying race, his energy and vitality gave him strength more in keeping with his picture of primitive man than with his own decadent heroes.

Witkacy's travels to the South Sea Islands had an effect beyond providing an exotic setting for several of his plays. His glimpses of the aborigines and the coral reefs and his personal contact with primitive societies influenced all his thinking about man's culture. Witkacy's attitudes to life and society are something experienced and felt, not simply intellectualized.

His anthropological journey with Malinowski enabled Witkacy to see Western civilization from the outside and to approach its customs and its natives as something as strange as anything New Guinea could offer. Subsequently Witkacy draws analogies between the petty tribal chieftains of the Papuans and the rulers of Europe and studies the common origins of strongmen and power politics the world over. From the perspective of the Australian bush, he perceives the relativity of all values and all ethical systems—civilization is simply a game. "Ethics is only the consequence of a large number of people thinking the same way. A man on a desert island wouldn't have any notion of what it means," the hero of *The Water Hen* declares.

A tribal squabble in another hemisphere at the opposite end of the world, the outbreak of the First World War on July 28, 1914, brought the expedition with Malinowski to a premature end. As an Austrian subject, Malinowski was interned in Australia and was then allowed to proceed with his anthropological studies. Despite the fact that the elder Witkiewicz had moved from Warsaw to Zakopane in the Austrian sector twenty-four years before, neither he nor his son had ever changed from Russian to Austrian citizenship. Witkacy was sent from Australia to Saint Petersburg; and here begins the third and by far the most important of his travels—the journey to Russia and through the Revolution.

Russia

Although only sons were exempt from military service in Russia at that time, Witkacy entered an officer's training school to avoid having to serve as an ordinary soldier later on when there was general conscription. Further, still stunned by his fiancée's suicide, he seemed indifferent to whatever happened to him and readily threw himself into the turmoil around him. Through an uncle's influence, he was commissioned an infantry officer in a regiment of the Imperial Life Guard. He was sent to the front in 1915, wounded at the battle of Molodechno, and decorated for bravery.

Witkacy remained in Russia until after the armistice and the formation of the new independent Polish state in 1918. He experienced many of the crucial events of the Russian Revolution firsthand, "swimming in the black sea of a mob gone mad," and witnessed the creation of a revolutionary new society, as he had previously seen the creation of revolutionary new art in Paris. Creation and revolution—these are the two poles on which everything revolves for Witkacy: the destruction of the old, the ceaseless change and flux, the endless battle to create something new out of the void. From the Papuans to the Bolsheviks, from Australia to Saint Petersburg—such sudden displacements and strange juxtapositions of violent experience could not but deepen the sense of metaphysical wonder at the plurality of phenomena which Witkacy felt was the essence of life and art. From the bonfire in Australia to the larger flames in Petersburg, Witkacy circled the globe in such a way as to make men seem insects in relation to infinity. "People are like insects, and Infinity surrounds them and summons them in a mysterious voice," observes the precocious small son in *The Water Hen.*

The Russian journey was rich in experience. More astounding even than the adventure with the ticks and the aborigines—and a further proof of his popularity with "natives"—was the fact that Witkacy was elected political commissar by the soldiers of his regiment after the revolution had started. He lived through one of the crucial moments of history from both sides; the collapse of the Russian Empire became his model for the disintegration of the whole world that he knew and of which he was a part. As an officer in the Tsarist army, Witkacy heard the last gasps of the *ancien régime;* then, as political commissar, he watched the subterranean forces burst forth from below.

The effect of these experiences on his art is incalculable. In virtually all his plays Witkacy portrays a crumbling world perched on a volcano or on an earthquake fault; tottering from the start, ready to collapse at the slightest push, this old order is doomed and dangerous. As the play unfolds, the tension mounts; the first tremors are felt, the eruption begins, and by the end of the last act there is either chaos or something new and frightening thrust up out of the upheaval. The excitement of a Witkacy play springs from the fact that history, both personal and world, is out of control; it works by dynamite.

> Everything in history has to blow up and can't move smoothly into the future along the well-greased tracks of reason. . . . No one individual is going to come up with a new utopia—the new social order will come about all by itself, by spontaneous combustion, explosion, eruption, forged out of the dialectical struggle of everyone's guts in the human boiler; we're sitting on the lid [*The Shoemakers*].

During his time in the fashionable regiment of the Imperial Guard, Witkacy threw himself into the decadent life of the upper classes and participated in the last days of the old depravity and intellectualism. He experimented with life and with art, taking cocaine and peyote for the first time and becoming involved in the excitement over abstract art. In Moscow he saw more Picasso. He began studying philosophy and aesthetics seriously and started to formulate his own ideas about modern art. He painted portraits of his fellow officers in the regiment and soon was selling them to make money for the expenses such a life entailed.

At the same time, Witkacy saw the rottenness and inequities of this world and knew that the masses would tear it down and reduce everything to the same level. He had long believed that Western civilization was in its final stages and that revolution was necessary and unavoidable, but that its tragic corollary was the subordination of the individual to society and the coming "dusk of mechanized grayness." The Russian Revolution convinced him that the greatest happiness of the greatest numbers meant total social conformity, and with it the end of the world to which he belonged and the destruction of the individual. For the author of *The Shoemakers*, the only hope for mankind lies in the regeneration of all of society and of the entire human race—the creation of a new species of man.

Yet despite his contempt for the new anthill society and his worship of individuality, Witkiewicz never romanticized the past or idealized strong men of any age; he was not a believer in an aristocratic elite or in fascist or totalitarian techniques for regenerating mankind. He remained skeptical and ironic about schemes for the rapid transformation of mankind, although he was sympathetic to radical change and felt it was necessary if man was to survive. If he was hostile to communism and feared its leveling effects, he despised the existing regime and regarded liberal democracy as a fraud and capitalism as a cancer on the body politic.

In his personal attitudes and behavior, Witkacy was generous and free from religious and racial prejudice. In the 1930's he befriended the Jewish writer Bruno Schulz, whose work he influenced, and helped him get his stories published. Nor was Witkacy a snob; his natural informality and man-to-man directness obliterated class distinctions. After he completed *The Shoemakers*, he read the play aloud to a group of specially invited guests: his maid, two neighborhood shoemakers, and a couple of young university students, one of whom was Jan Kott. As for the superman, the hero of *The Cuttlefish* (1922) exposes the fraudulent pose of his antagonist Hyrkan IV and kills him just before the play ends.

> You're only great given the extremely low level of civilization in your country. Nowadays Nietzsche's superman can't be anything more than a small-time thug. And those who would have been rulers in the past are the artists of our own times. Breeding the superman is the biggest hoax I've ever heard of.

Witkacy maintained a dialectical view of the relation between the individual and society which is one of his strengths as a dramatist, even if it led him to a position of despair and defeat in his personal views. He can argue both sides and be critical of each, seeing the defects of each position: on the one hand, the arrogant individualist isolated in his power and privilege, and, on the other, the faceless millions reduced to so many cogs and spokes in the wheels of society, which turn without their conviction or consent.

Out of these unresolved and unresolvable oppositions grows Witkacy's apocalyptic vision of life: there are no choices left, there is no way out. In *The Anonymous Work*, "Four Acts of a Rather Nasty Nightmare" (1921), the hero Plazmonik cannot identify with either side in a revolution that is neither entirely right or entirely wrong and decides to go back to prison and spend the rest of his days there: "In our times there are only two places for metaphysical individuals, prison or the insane asylum."

Witkacy is a product of the Russian Revolution. As a result of his personal and historical experiences, he acquired a prophetic sense of the ideological conflicts that came to dominate European history in the next forty years and still obsess us today. "I like you because of the seismograph you carry around in your head," the locomotive engineer Tenser tells his fireman Nicholas in *The Crazy Locomotive;* "you don't even know it's there, but all the time it's recording obscure tremors." Witkacy had a seismograph in his head attuned to the tremors of history. He had a terrible presentiment of the disaster and catastrophe

that would overtake all of Europe; in his plays and novels he foresaw
the future as dissolution and destruction.

CREATION

Witkacy the artist was born in revolutionary Russia.[7] His creativity
as a painter and writer bursts forth like an explosion as a result of living
through that shattering upheaval. When he returned home from his
Russian journey in 1918, he came back to a new creation—Poland, a
country which had not existed for over a hundred years and had only
now become a modern state as a result of the Treaty of Versailles.
From this point on, the ex-Russian officer and commissar became
Witkacy, superartist from Zakopane, turning out dozens of plays,
paintings by the cartload, hundreds of articles on art, literature, and
philosophy, two vast novels, an original aesthetic theory of painting and
theater, an existentialist philosophy, and miscellaneous writings on demonism and drugs. In the period between the two wars—from the time
he was thirty-two years old until his self-inflicted death at the age of
fifty-four—Witkacy produced a series of improvised masterpieces in
the many genres and forms of art which he pursued simultaneously. He
began his productive career relatively late, after years of dissipation and
adventure, and even then he was unable to settle down to any one art,
but threw himself into all at once. Like Leon in *The Mother*, he
remained something of a willful dilettante, a type he defended in an age
of overspecialization.

A Theater of Amateurs

From 1918 to 1926 Witkacy devoted much of his energies to the
theater and to the theory of the drama, writing over thirty plays and
developing an original poetics. His fertility is astounding. In 1920 he
wrote at least five plays, including *They*, and in 1921 he increased his
production to at least six, of which *The Water Hen* is the most famous.
It is impossible to be sure exactly how many plays Witkacy actually
wrote since most of them remained only in manuscript and many were
lost during the ravages of the Second World War.

Of the thirty plays Witkacy wrote during this eight-year period,
only seven were ever published in his lifetime, and the dozen or so that
were staged were given occasional performances, most often by ama-
teurs, and received little favorable critical comment. We know by title
only eleven plays which were presumably destroyed in the holocaust;
others have been discovered and recovered due to the efforts of Kon-

[7] Andrzej Mencwel, "Witkacego jedność w wielości" ("Witkacy's Unity in
Plurality"), *Dialog*, No. 12 (December, 1965), p. 85.

stanty Puzyna, who brought out the first edition of Witkacy's plays in 1962. *Sluts and Butterflies*, "A Comedy with Corpses in Two Acts" (1922), turned up for the first time as late as 1958; the text of *The Crazy Locomotive* (1923) had to be pieced together from two different French translations since the Polish original is lost; and *The Terrible Tutor* (1920) survives in only two of four acts. The thought that one of the lost plays (with titles like *A Superfluous Man, Hangover,* and *The Baleful Bastard of Vermiston*) may still be found in an attic somewhere in the south of Sicily or in an old sea chest in a fishing ship off the coast of Madagascar is an intriguing Witkacian possibility.

Except by a coterie of friends, Witkacy was not taken seriously as a dramatist in his own time, but rather was regarded as an eccentric dilettante and decadent practical joker out to *épater les bourgeois* with absurd titles, preposterous characters and settings, and wildly incoherent plots and dialogue. Witkacy attempted to stage some of his own plays in Zakopane and established the Formist Theater in the ballroom of the Sea Watch, the most expensive hotel in town. However, the local paper, the *Voice of Zakopane,* and the public at large were hostile to these efforts. The casts were amateur, and Witkacy himself designed the scenery and directed. A contemporary has described the spirit of these productions:

> Witkacy's theater was amateur in the true sense of the word. Those who acted in it were dentists and painters, government weather forecasters, that is, employees of the National Meteorological Institute, and women with green eyes. Most important of all were those who spoke Polish with difficulty, with an English, Byelorussian, or Russian accent.[8]

In 1926 the actors in a Warsaw theater simply refused to take part in the production of *Tumor Brainard,* and the play had to be withdrawn. Witkacy's theater was appreciated only by a few of the most intelligent critics, notably by Tadeusz Boy-Żeleński, the poet, critic, and translator who is mentioned a number of times by Witkacy in *The Shoemakers.* Boy characterized Witkacy's theater as metaphysical buffoonery and supercabaret, presenting the sadness, boredom, and despair of modern civilization with a spasmodic laugh. However, most audiences found the plays incomprehensible and the author mad or at least on the verge of madness. As a playwright, Witkacy was a quarter of a century ahead of his time; not until after the revolution brought about by Beckett and Ionesco in the 1950's did such a vision and such dramaturgy become acceptable to even the sophisticated spectator.

[8] Rafał Malczewski, quoted in Konstanty Puzyna, "Nota" ("Appendix"), in *Dramaty,* by S. I. Witkiewicz (Warsaw: Panstwowy Instytut Wydawniczy, 1962), II, 638–39.

Toward the end of the 1920's, discouraged by lack of understanding, Witkacy virtually abandoned playwriting, returning to drama for the last time in the mid-thirties with *The Shoemakers*, a work more somber in outlook than his other plays, and different in technique. Witkacy complained bitterly and blamed both the public and the critics for their stupidity.

In my opinion the position of artists here in our country is, with a few exceptions, extremely bad. The basic attitude of our society toward those who create something new in art is hostile. If they are not treated as enemies (supposedly) of all constructive patriotic social values, and as enemies of art (conceived as realism) which really isn't art at all, they are at best treated· as harmless buffoons who can at least be ridiculed. The blame for this must also fall on the shoulders of the critics who are not at all interested in artistic problems and who don't want to learn anything about them, as can be shown by the reaction to my theoretical works (*New Forms in Painting* and *Aesthetic Sketches*) and the controversy about my book entitled *The Theater*. Putting aside for the moment the question of the critics' lack of training in aesthetics, their greatest fault is their inability to follow an argument logically, which makes it impossible to carry on a discussion with them and renders the fight fruitless. In the old days a Polish artist could at least count on his death to bring him recognition. But since the death of Tadeusz Miciński, who was forgotten in spite of it, it is clear that such a comparatively speaking risky experiment does not have the desired results any more.[9]

Tadeusz Miciński was a symbolist poet and expressionist dramatist and novelist, whose plays and novels with their imaginative mixture of different epochs and countries had great influence on Witkacy. They were both in Russia during the war and visited art galleries together. Witkacy refers to Miciński and his play *Basilissa Teophan* (1909) frequently in his own works, and Miciński's bizarre death and lack of recognition haunted him and served as an example of the grotesque workings of the world: Miciński was killed in 1918 in Russia, as he was returning home, by an irate mob who took him for a tsarist general.

The S. I. Witkiewicz Portrait-Painting Firm

Even during the period of Witkacy's greatest creativity in the drama, it was not as a playwright that he was best known, but as a painter and aesthetician. While rapidly tossing off thirty plays as an amateur, he made his living as a portrait painter and devoted his professional energies to art. Here he was even more productive than in

---

[9] "Interview with S. I. Witkiewicz," *Wiadomości Literackie* ("Literary News"), No. 15, 1924. Quoted in the program of Teatr Polski, Warsaw, No. 24, season 1965–66, p. 8.

the drama, regarding much of his work in painting not as art, but simply as a job and a means of earning his living. His total output in landscapes and portraits probably runs into the thousands. In 1916 alone, while he was in Saint Petersburg and discovering what a profitable business painting could be, he is reputed to have turned out over two hundred portraits at the same time that he was carrying out his duties as an officer. The large exhibition of his paintings in Cracow in 1967 consisting of 261 canvases and drawings showed only a fraction of his work. Many of the portraits were lost during the Second World War, others have never been identified, and still others are scattered about the world in private homes from Warsaw to Berkeley, California.

His portraits became popular with the well-to-do, especially in Cracow and Warsaw, and the demand was great. From 1923 Witkacy approached much of his portrait painting as a money-making industry, and he finally printed a prospectus called *The Rules of the S. I. Witkiewicz Portrait-Painting Firm* (Warsaw, 1928, reissued in 1932), setting down the regulations governing those who commissioned him to paint their portraits. The Firm's motto was: "The customer must be satisfied. Misunderstandings are unimaginable."

The always-satisfied customers were required to make a down payment, usually one third of the total fee, before work on the portrait was begun, and to pay the rest when the portrait was completed. The number of sittings varied, but a great number of portraits were done by Witkacy at high speeds rivaling his own crazy locomotive. It was not at all unusual for him to finish a portrait in two or three hours. The Firm offered customers a choice among seven types of portraits, ranging from simple and complimentary to the sitter (Type A) to those containing more and more "character study" with accompanying deformation, elongation, and enhancement of particular features. Types C, C & Co, Et, C & H, C & Co & Et, and so on, were executed by the Firm with the help of quality narcotics, and the more expensive the drugs, the more expensive the portrait. The customer was free to choose whether he wanted a flattering portrait or a psychological study; even abstractions were available, as was feminine beautification that would make the subject appear more demonic.

According to the rules, the customer was not allowed to express any opinion about the work commissioned, although he was required to pay the fee whether he liked the finished product or not. Sometimes his customers, many of whom were wealthy society women, got into unpleasant quarrels with Witkacy when they found that their portraits were not sufficiently flattering and true to life. Faced with acrimonious protests, the painter either coaxed, remained utterly silent, or flew into a rage, depending on his mood. Paragraph 3 of the Firm's bylaws was designed to prevent such scenes, but did not always succeed.

Any kind of criticism on the part of the customer is *absolutely* ruled out. The customer may not like the portrait, but the Firm cannot permit even the slightest comment without a special dispensation. If the Firm had allowed itself the luxury of listening to the customers' views, it would have gone out of its mind a long time ago. WE PUT PARTICULAR STRESS ON THIS PARAGRAPH, SINCE IT IS EXTREMELY DIFFICULT TO RESTRAIN THE CUSTOMER FROM MAKING COMMENTS WHICH ARE REALLY QUITE UNCALLED FOR.

If the customer simply could not stand his completed portrait, he had the option of paying one third of the fee only and leaving the portrait behind as property of the Firm. What Witkacy wanted to avoid at all costs was too close human contact with his customers. As he explains in the final clause of Paragraph 3, "The Firm's nerves must be respected, considering how extremely difficult its job is." Paragraph 10 laid down further laws: "Customers have the obligation to show up for the sittings punctually, since waiting upsets the Firm and may have a negative influence on the execution of the work."

If Witkacy turned into the impersonal, legalistic Firm for his paying customers, a second group of people who sat for their portraits received a quite different kind of treatment. These were his friends and acquaintances, who did not have to pay anything for their pictures and who even had the right to argue with the painter about how he was depicting them. These friends simply donated their time to sitting for Witkacy and in return received free of charge not only a portrait, but hours of brilliant conversation full of characteristic Witkacian irony and self-depreciation.

In the first category of portraits, Witkacy was painting for money and turned out work that sometimes tended to be conventional and perfunctory; in the second category of paintings, he was working to please himself and his friends, and he felt free to indulge in experiments and to push creativity to its limits. In the mid-twenties Witkacy began to experiment with painting under the influence of drugs.

Nicotine, Alcohol, Cocaine, Peyote, Morphine, and Ether

Hundreds of the amazing portraits which he painted bear mysterious letters and numbers next to the signature; these symbols indicate the amounts and kinds of alcohol and drugs he took for each creative effort. Painting under the influence of drugs was one of Witkacy's many attempts to go beyond the normal bounds of everyday experience and to break through objective reality into the inner world of metaphysical feelings. The anguished distortion, terrifying colors, and broken lines of these portraits painted under the influence of drugs are uncontrolled plunges into the irrational. Like the surrealists at about the same time and Henri Michaux, André Masson, and many other artists since, Witkacy by his use of drugs as a creative stimulant wanted to bypass the will and intellect and tap the subconscious.

Witkacy may have needed drugs to go on creating at such an intense rate. In *The Madman and the Nun* (1923), the poet Walpurg explains why he took cocaine and morphine: "My nerves weren't strong enough to resist that damnable something or other that compelled me to write. I had to poison myself. I had to gain strength." Like Walpurg, Witkacy lived at the edge of his nerves, without any sense of moderation, not conserving his strength, but trying desperately to expend it to the full at every moment of his life. Drugs made it possible for him to live and create beyond the limits of his strength and to perceive the universe with heightened intensity. Narcotics were a liberation from normal vision, a mystical experience, a derangement of the senses that revealed inner reality—the world of Pure Form. Morphine and cocaine enabled him to depict, not the accurate head of cabbage his father championed, but a world of fantasy and madness.

Despite his experiments with drugs, Witkacy does not see the liberation they provide as anything but a dangerous delusion. As usual, he grasps both sides of the situation dramatically and presents the negative consequences with great force. Drug addiction figures in many of Witkacy's works whose heroes often hope to transcend reality and achieve instant happiness and perfection through narcotics and pills. In plays like *The Madman and the Nun* and *The Mother*, addiction is linked to insanity and ends in self-destruction. The cocaine party in *The Mother*, which leads to a disruption of normal spatial and temporal relationships and allows the characters a glimpse of a fourth dimension of reality, is presented as something grotesque and frightening—the vision it produces is a nightmare.

Rather than offering a solution to the overwhelming metaphysical questions: What sense does anything make? Why are things the way they are and not some other way? Who am I? Why do I exist?—drugs and pills simply lull our basic human anxieties to sleep like those other "drugs," the various social and political "isms," or else create still worse insatiability. Witkacy's interest in drugs and pills is again prophetic. Since all of life is becoming artificial and synthetic, he fears that the authentic human response to the universe will be replaced by the ersatz and automated. In *Sluts and Butterflies, or The Green Pill,* "A Comedy with Corpses in Two Acts and Three Scenes" (1922), one of the demonic heroines explains the new discovery: "Pills—that's the ultimate mystery . . . We have a new drug which creates such an awful insatiable craving that Messalina would be a perfect angel in comparison to the addicts who'll take it."

In this play the white race, civilized but impotent, has to resort to pills to survive; the savage primitive race of Mandelbaums (the cast of characters includes forty characters all named Mandelbaum, of various sizes and ages) living in the tropics proves superior to the degenerate, drug-addicted Europeans. Pills and drugs are mechanical substitutes designed to render unnecessary the genuine feelings, purposes, and beliefs which have been destroyed in the chaotic absurdity of twentieth-century civilization. In his works, Witkacy does not romanticize drugs or drug addicts, nor does he present pills and stimulants as the solution to the loss of meaning in our lives. These are at best desperate artifices, usually leading to disaster; at worst they can be sinister tools in the hands of the secret forces working to reduce mankind to mechanized docility.

Witkacy the drug addict is another aspect of the legend which he himself helped to perpetuate. In 1932 he published a book entitled *Nicotine, Alcohol, Cocaine, Peyote, Morphine, and Ether*, describing his experiences with drugs and stimulants and the advantages to be had from each. Cocaine appears to have been his favorite.

Pure Form

Throughout the 1920's, concurrent with his work as dramatist, painter, and novelist, Witkacy the critic and aesthetician was busy battling the artistic and cultural establishment and arguing for his own theory of Pure Form in painting and drama. He wrote dozens of polemic articles defending his own works and ideas for various literary weeklies and journals and developed his own aesthetic theory in *New Forms in Painting* in 1919, *Aesthetic Sketches* in 1922, and *An Introduction to the Theory of Pure Form in the Theater* in 1923.

Upon his return to Poland from Russia, Witkacy became a member of a group of painters and writers called the Formists. This group had an important influence on the development of Witkiewicz' aesthetic theory, especially Leon Chwistek and his doctrine of the plurality of realities, to which there are many references in the plays. Chwistek (1884–1944) was the son of a Zakopane doctor and, like his friend Witkacy, a genius of many talents. He was a mathematical logician, philosopher, aesthetician, essayist, and painter. His theory of realities, developed in *The Plurality of Realities* (1921) and *The Plurality of Realities in Art*, criticized the idea of a single, uniform reality and postulated four different realities: (1) the reality of natural objects; (2) the reality of matter as studied in physics; (3) the reality of impressions and appearances; and (4) the reality of images created by us. Applied to aesthetics, these four different realities produce four different kinds of art: (1) primitive art where each object is given its own basic primary color; (2) realism where the physical reality of a particular time and place is depicted; (3) impressionism in which sensations are treated psychologically; and (4) futurism or expressionism in which free images are fantastically created. According to Chwistek's theory of formism, the artist is only obliged to give perfect form to what he has created—each style is equally valid. The form, not the reality portrayed, is all that can be judged.

Witkacy's pure form is closely related to Chwistek's formism. Further, his plays are based on the notion of the plurality of realities and the corresponding modes of depicting each. Often a single play will shift from one reality to another and move from one style to another, taking the spectator on a jolting ride into new dimensions, as in *The Madman and the Nun* or *The Mother* in which we go from the psychological impressionism of the early acts to the fantastic expressionism of the denouements. The plurality of realities is also one of the prime sources of the metaphysical feeling of the strangeness of existence, attacking as it does the whole idea of one's own unity and identity.

Bafflement in the face of an inexplicable universe is the metaphysical feeling which Witkacy claimed the theater should arouse in the audience. In *An Introduction to the Theory of Pure Form in the Theater*, Witkacy proposes a new kind of play which will be liberated from the confines of imitating life and instead make a synthesis of all the elements of the theater—sound, setting, gesture, dialogue—for purely formal ends. Freed from the demands of consistent psychology and logic, the dramatist will be able to use his materials as the musician uses notes and the modern painter colors and shapes. The meaning of such a work lies in its internal construction, not in the discursive content of its subject matter. We are transported into an entirely new world that is free and unpredictable.

> On leaving the theater, the spectator ought to have the feeling that he has just awakened from some strange dream, in which even the most ordinary things had a strange, unfathomable charm, characteristic of dream reveries, and unlike anything else in the world.

Since human beings are the chief elements in drama, Witkacy maintained that theater can never be perfectly abstract like the pure arts of painting and music. The form may be pure, but the materials are the impure facts of life in the twentieth century. The elements of reality are present in Pure Form, but transposed into a new dimension. Ever since his Russian adventures, art was for Witkacy the expression of metaphysical feelings, and not the presentation of reality through either naturalistic means or symbols. Form and content were inseparable.

Witkacy's heretical views kept him constantly engaged in controversy. He was outspoken in his rejection of the two respected "isms" of his day, realism and symbolism. "I'm not condemning either realistic painting or realistic theater—I'm simply saying *it is not art*," he wrote in the *Zakopane Voice* in 1925 at a time when he was trying to stage his own plays in the local theaters.[10] The older generation totally failed to understand his position and regarded him as the brash, irresponsible son of a distinguished father.

It was not only Witkacy's views on art which aroused the hostility and suspicion, and sometimes the metaphysical wonder, of his elders and contemporaries. His life seemed an experiment in Pure Form. His demonic poses, his eccentric habits, and his disdain for social conformity made him the source of much curiosity and the subject of many anecdotes.

Signs over the door of his Zakopane apartment gave detailed information about exactly when he would receive different tradesmen and when he would see his friends: from 3:30 to 4:00 A.M. for his tailor, from 4:00 to 4:30 A.M. for the butcher, and so on. Apparently no one paid any attention to these rules, least of all Witkacy himself. When he did receive guests, he was often in his bathrobe or stark naked. He collected walking sticks that had belonged to famous men (perhaps his response to his father's hobby of mountain climbing) and love letters and other amorous materials. He had an album of what he called "curiosities," including mementos from Australia, an autographed picture of the young Artur Rubinstein, and Rita Sacchetto's garter. He was accused of being a sex maniac and of appearing drunk when he lectured on art, philosophy, and literature.

His dealings with his friends were often tempestuous. He assigned each of his friends a number to indicate where this individual stood in his esteem at any given moment, and he kept a running record of the standings. If a friend did something that displeased Witkacy, he would be informed that he had been dropped from position 17 to position 88 as punishment; other, temporarily favored friends would be advanced into more coveted places. Along with the rules of the Portrait Painting Firm and the signs above his door, Witkacy's ranking of his friends in a constantly shifting order of priority indicates his fondness for playing games. He also liked to stage situations in which total strangers would be brought together purposely so that he could guide the conversation along some previously planned and appropriately mysterious course

[10] Puzyna, "Nota," p. 638.

that would completely baffle the participants. He delighted in making private jokes when he was out in company, bewildering the majority of guests who had no idea what he was talking about.

His fondness for playing games and his desire to impose some bizarre personal order on the world, or perhaps to transform life into a game, are part of the fundamental inspiration for his plays and a source of their originality and spontaneity. Pure Form is another such invented system. In the Preface to his play *The Marriage* (1946) Witold Gombrowicz, who carries on the Witkacy tradition in both drama and fiction, refers to the world he is depicting as "this world of games and eternal artifices, of eternal imitations and mystifications." [11]

Witkacy never outgrew the world of games and mystifications. Rather than a source of weakness, his refusal to take the theater altogether seriously, his flippant attitude to his own medium, his indulgence in self-parody and self-irony, and his treatment of art as a stunt and an extended gag help to give his plays much of their contemporary flavor. In this respect his work has much in common with Jarry's *Ubu the King*, the schoolboy prank with which modern avant-garde drama starts.

Life and art have both become too preposterous to take seriously—they can only be treated as burlesque, parody, and mystification. At the end of *The Water Hen*, as grenades explode and machine-gun fire can be heard, the Father organizes a card game; in the face of protests from his friends, he explains: "It's the only way of whiling away the time during a social upheaval. What else could we do?"

Novels

By the latter half of the 1920's Witkacy had virtually abandoned the theater and pure form and created a new artistic role and personality for himself, that of novelist or rather antinovelist, since he regarded the novel as outside the realm of art and a kind of grab bag into which the most heterogeneous material could be stuffed. He had already written *Bung's Downfall 622 Times, or a Demonic Woman* in 1910, an unpublished and unfinished work. Now he produced two vast works of fantastic fiction, *Farewell to Autumn* (begun in 1925, published in 1927) and *Insatiability* (1930), both of which portray the collapse of Western civilization in nightmare visions of the future where the sexual, political, and philosophical are grotesquely intermingled. [12]

---

[11] Witold Gombrowicz, *Théâtre* (Paris: Julliard, 1965), p. 88. Gombrowicz refers to Witkiewicz and his theory of Pure Form in the Preface to *The Marriage*.

[12] We are indebted to Czeslaw Milosz' discussion of Witkiewicz' novels in *The Captive Mind*, chap. i, "The Pill of Murti-Bing" (New York: Alfred A. Knopf, 1963), pp. 3–24, and in "S. I. Witkiewicz, a Polish Writer for Today," pp. 143–54.

Witkacy was indeed insatiable in his pursuit of new artistic forms, and in the nonart form of the novel he found a perfect receptacle into which to pour satire, literary criticism, philosophical treatises, footnotes, personal invective, digressions of every sort, apocalyptic visions of disaster, and all kinds of verbal games, ironies, and parodies reducing the novel form itself to absurdity. The characters' names continue the multilingual anagrams and crossword puzzles found also in the cast of characters in the plays. The style is a bizarre mixture of philosophical language, polyglot puns, exaggerated grandiosity, invented words, and convoluted syntax. The world portrayed is the decadent artistic and intellectual circle on the verge of collapse; religion and philosophy are dead, art is growing more and more perverse and insane.

In *Farewell to Autumn,* two revolutions take place, the first bourgeois-liberal; the second, totalitarian, reducing all to the same level and bringing about universal grayness and social mechanization. The hero Atanazy Bazakbal, a would-be artist, comes home from India at the time of the revolution, becomes a petty functionary, and like Leon in *The Mother* becomes obsessed with the seemingly irreversible process of socialization which is destroying the individual and the mystery of life. After taking cocaine, he decides to escape across the mountains near Zakopane, but finally returns to alert others to their plight and to the necessity of doing something about it. He is shot at the border as a spy.

Insatiability presents an even more phantasmogoric picture of times to come, in which the world is divided up into warring factions dominated by different ideologies. Communist China is threatening to conquer all of Europe, having already taken over Russia. Witkacy's usual group of neurotic artists and demonic women suffers from a total sense of futility and metaphysical insatiability and is unable to do anything to resist the coming catastrophe. At this point, mysterious vendors start selling a magic pill, devised by the Malayan-Chinese philosopher Murti-Bing and called the Murti-Bing pill. The pill is a condensed form of the philosophy that has made the Sino-Mongolian army so successful; it brings perfect contentment and makes all metaphysical questioning disappear. More and more people take the pill and become converted to Murti-Bingism, which solves all their problems and lulls their anxieties. Ultimately the armies of the East occupy the West after the surrender of the Western general, and Murti-Bingism triumphs. The old neurotic heroes no longer write dissonant modern music but joyful marches and no longer paint abstractions but socially useful pictures, all under the auspices of the Ministry of the Mechanization of Culture.

Witkacy deplored all substitutes for metaphysics, whether a pill or a materialistic totalitarian philosophy. Mankind looked for answers to the basic questions about existence first in religion, then in philosophy and art. Religion was dead, philosophy was dying. Only art survived to deal with metaphysical questions, but, cut off from the once orderly picture of the universe formerly supplied by religion and philosophy, art could no longer be harmonious. As a substitute for religion and philosophy, modern art was forced to go to greater and greater extremes and artists were driven to madness in their quest to satisfy man's metaphysical longings. Modern artists were the last spokesmen for the old world of suffering from metaphysical anguish; soon they would be put into insane asylums. Socialization would turn theaters into foundling homes for retarded children. The new social order would make all mankind happy, without religion, without philosophy, without art. These are the two extreme positions: art grows more and more desperately mad; the forces for social mechanization and conformity become more and more powerful. Only philosophy could save mankind, and philosophy was bankrupt.

> Every epoch has the philosophy it deserves. In our present phase we deserve nothing better than a drug of the most inferior kind, to lull to sleep our metaphysical anxiety which hinders our transformation into automatic machines.[13]

Philosophy and Shoemakers

Discouraged by lack of interest in and understanding of his theories, plays, and novels, in the face of frustration and defeat and increasingly disastrous forebodings of what was soon going to happen to civilization, Witkacy gradually withdrew from the world, abandoned literature, and devoted more and more of his time and energies to a new role and a new game: philosophy. Like Edgar in *The Water Hen*, Witkacy was a man always desperately searching for a new career and an ultimate meaning: "I should have been somebody, but I never knew what, or rather who." Philosophy more than art or anything else seemed capable of providing answers and solutions.

Witkacy took philosophy more seriously than either fiction or drama. He was fascinated by logic and logicians and corresponded with many, both Polish and foreign, including men like Edmund Husserl and Rudolf Carnap, and he attended many philosophical congresses. Although his interest in philosophy went back to his stay in Russia and he began working on his major philosophical work as early as 1917, Witkacy only began to devote his full attention to the subject late in

---

[13] S. I. Witkiewicz, quoted by Czeslaw Milosz in "S. I. Witkiewicz, a Polish Writer for Today," p. 146.

life, as a nonprofessional without any formal training and discipline. He was aware of his amateur status and commented on it ironically; in a lecture at Zakopane, attended by the local intellectual elite and visitors from Cracow and Warsaw, many of them professors, Witkacy called attention to the fact that he was a man without a university degree lecturing to professionals.

In academic and professional philosophical circles he was most often patronized as a self-taught dilettante, despite his vast reading in Russian, German, French, and English, as well as Polish. On the other hand, two important philosophers who knew Witkacy at this period, Tadeusz Kotarbiński and Roman Ingarden, esteemed him highly as a thinker. Ingarden points out that Witkacy was concerned with different issues from the technical logical problems with which Polish philosophy was preoccupied at that time.

> Why was Witkiewicz valuable in our philosophical milieu? Did he stand out by the range of his philosophical education? Was he better than the others by the precision of his reasoning and his exactness in formulating results? It seems to me that in these respects he was not an equal of his various peers, particularly those younger than himself, professionally trained philosophers from the Lvov or the Warsaw school. . . . And yet—this is my firm conviction—he was more of a philosopher than many of those who looked down their noses at him, treating him at best as a philosophizing literary critic, and not a scholar.[14]

Ingarden goes on to praise Witkacy as an existentialist philosopher long before Sartre.

> He was in all of this, in his fundamental position, an existentialist many years before the movement appeared in France, and was probably contemporary with Heidegger. But, so far as I know, he never read Heidegger. So far as phenomenologists are concerned, he knew only Husserl's *Logische Untersuchungen*, but the problems of the philosophical bases of logic he never considered essential, and he also had no understanding of phenomenological analyses. He differed from the French existentialists—despite his profound pessimism—because he had more elemental dynamism and primordial autogeny, and philosophically he had greater ambitions to create a complete metaphysical system.[15]

[14] Roman Ingarden, "Wspomnienie o Witkacym" ("My Reminiscences about Witkacy"), in *S. I. Witkiewicz, człowiek i twórca*, Commemorative Volume edited by Tadeusz Kotarbiński and Jerzy E. Płomieński (Warsaw: Panstwowy Instytut Wydawniczy, 1957), p. 173.

[15] *Ibid.*, p. 175 fn.

In 1935 Witkacy published his only book of philosophy, *Concepts and Principles Implied by the Concept of Existence*, which he had been working on for years and which represented the summation of his philosophical studies beginning at the time of the Russian Revolution. He continued writing articles on philosophical subjects and publishing widely in scholarly journals until his death.

Concepts and Principles is a work of technical philosophy in which Witkacy attempts to solve a whole series of philosophic problems—mostly metaphysical, but also epistemological—in a systematic way. His aim is to develop a single coherent system, and his essential position is pluralist, in the manner of Aristotle and somewhat reminiscent of John Dewey, rather than monistic (Spinoza, Hegel) or even dualist (Descartes). As a philosopher, Witkacy is fundamentally a realist, rather than an idealist. Although he uses the term "improved monadology," there is really little of Leibniz in *Concepts and Principles*, except for the pluralism, since there is interaction among existences. In his approach to philosophy, Witkacy is a talented eclectic attracted by the tough-minded, rather than by the romantic, tender-hearted philosophers.

Witkacy remained an amateur all his life in the sense that he cultivated philosophy and the arts to satisfy his own personal needs. He was bound to no one particular school of thought, nor to any single discipline. In everything he did he concerned himself with the fundamental problem of existence and its meaning, trying to encompass all the fields of human endeavor and to comprehend the totality of life.

From 1933, Witkacy lived more and more in isolation in the mountains at Zakopane where he pursued his work on philosophy. His only imaginative work from this period, *The Shoemakers* (1931–34), reflects his growing pessimism and sense of defeat. "A Theoretical Play with Songs," *The Shoemakers* is like his novels in spirit and technique, an abandonment of pure form for a more direct assault on the world around him by means of a fantastic hodgepodge of political and philosophical arguments, rhetoric, literary parody, comments on his friends, jokes in mock Russian, invented insults and obscenities, imaginary menus, and frightening prophecies of disaster.

Much more than the Pure Form plays, *The Shoemakers* reflects directly Witkacy's own times, the political situation in Poland, and the rise of totalitarian dictatorships in Europe. In his artistic development, Witkacy moves from the esoteric pursuit of pure form in art with its promise of a new cultural era to a bitter denunciation of the present which no art, pure or otherwise, can redeem, and which is culturally and politically doomed. His belief in the power of the human intellect to arrest the disastrous course of history has been destroyed by what he sees around him.

In *The Shoemakers* all causes and philosophies prove impotent and in their profusion cancel one another out; every belief contains its opposite, and parody and irony undermine faith in the very bases of life in such a world. The humor in Witkacy's last play has grown corrosive and self-destructive; *The Shoemakers* turns into a frightening mockery of everything, including the audience, the author, and the drama. A sign saying BOREDOM appears several times in the last act—the playwright is destroying the form of the drama, writing an antiplay that is the end of the line. Throughout his career, Witkacy had thrown himself desperately into creation as a battle against the void—like so many of his heroes, he had wanted to play himself out. Now he began to lose faith even in this possibility.

Witkacy's growing gloom was by no means simply a personal neurosis; he was concerned with deteriorating conditions in Europe and deeply disturbed by the spread of fascism. "What awaits us is one gigantic concentration camp," he predicted.[16] His whole life and work had been dedicated to individuality, freedom, creativity, and the expansion of the human mind; he saw that all of this would be destroyed and that he was powerless to do anything about it.

In late 1938, he was one of a group of distinguished guests at a private party in Warsaw. The occasion was the conferring of an honorary degree from a German University on a Polish scholar. At this time an intellectual flirtation was going on between the German ambassador von Moltke and some Polish intellectuals and university professors, and von Moltke was treated with much more deference than the state of affairs in Europe warranted. Witkacy listened to the billing and cooing as long as he could, and then turned to a friend next to him and said: "Either I'll have to get up and scream that this is disgraceful—or I'll have to go into the other room and take some cocaine." On the advice of his friend, Witkacy followed the latter course, impotent to stop the catastrophe he knew was coming soon by an outburst of temper, falling back on drugs to pacify his anger and anguish.

His friend Jerzy Płomieński, coeditor with Kotarbiński of the memorial volume of 1957 devoted to Witkiewicz, describes their last meeting in Zakopane toward the end of August, 1939, a few days before the war and only a few weeks before Witkacy's suicide. Witkacy was nervous and pessimistic; his face was haggard and gaunt. He

---

[16] Jerzy E. Płomieński, "Polski *pontifex maximus* katastrofizmu" ("The Polish *Pontifex Maximus* of Catastrophism"), in *S. I. Witkiewicz, człowiek i twórca*, p. 265.

pointed through the window toward the Tatra mountains and said that
he would have to leave all this very soon. He then began to talk about
the war that was imminent and dwelt at length on the horrors the war
would bring.

> You can't even imagine the kind of hell that's about to fall on our heads.
> Few of us will live through it. Not one stone will remain standing that
> our generation and our age knew as its own. We are a new Atlantis
> which the wild flood will engulf with all our theories, theories which
> failed to master life and discover its mysterious mechanism accurately
> enough, with all our hysterical forebodings of disaster, too refined and
> sterile, like all this decadent era of ours, a cursed era, with its
> *Schöngeist* hopelessly inadequate for man in the modern world. I feel I
> am nearing the end, together with this era.[17]

An aristocratic superman who ridiculed supermen and realized the
aristocracy had outlived its day, a Renaissance man who knew the Renaissance was long over, a prolific creator who did not believe in the
powers of creation, a flamboyant individualist who knew the individual
would be swallowed up in the social revolutions that must destroy the
rotten old order to institute the mechanized world of the future:
Witkiewicz was a tragic victim of his times, viewing even his own
self-irony ironically, with belief in neither past, present, nor future. For
almost fifty years he had driven himself to create, so as not to face the
ultimate horror, absurdity, and despair.

When the war broke out on September 1, 1939, Witkiewicz was in
Warsaw. Along with many others, he left the capital and moved
toward the eastern provinces where the second line of resistance was to
be organized against the Germans. On September 17, the Russians
crossed the border claiming the eastern provinces which before the
First World War had been part of the tsarist empire. On September
18, Witkiewicz killed himself; he took sleeping pills in a forest, woke
up and cut his wrists with a razor, against a magnificent natural background as in *Farewell to Autumn*.[18] His last words, spoken to a woman
who was with him at the end, were in Russian: "*Ya ne budu zhit' pod
merku*" ("I won't go on living as less than myself").

In his apartment in Warsaw he left behind a chest full of essays and
plays, all of which were presumably lost during the war when the city
was razed to the ground by the Germans. The title of one of these
plays destroyed during the holocaust was *The End of the World*.

---

[17] *Ibid.*, p. 264.
[18] Czeslaw Milosz, "S. I. Witkiewicz, a Polish Writer for Today," p. 153.

EPILOGUE

If the story ended there, it would be possible to say that Witkiewicz died a frustrated and tragic victim of his own and of his age's violent, self-destructive impulses. He would be nothing more than a might-have-been, who anticipated by a generation the theater of the absurd and the theater of cruelty, but who drew an unlucky number in the lottery of history and had the misfortune of being a Pole—he would never come into his own as an artist. In fact, for many years after his death it seemed highly improbable that his bizarre works would ever be anything but a curiosity for a select group of connoisseurs, especially in Poland after the socialist revolution.

However, Witkacy was never content with conventional tragic endings, and his own story has, like many of his own plays, a fantastic epilogue where the principal character, seemingly dead, comes back to life and proves to his disparagers that he is full of vitality. Like Walpurg, dead by his own hand, Witkacy suddenly re-enters with a yellow flower in his buttonhole to become a major force in the modern Polish avant-garde and from there to be recognized in Europe and America as one of the giants of twentieth-century experimental theater.

But it took another revolution to make this possible. As long as socialist realism held sway in Poland, Witkiewicz remained a forgotten figure, but with the October revolution of 1956, the Polish theater returned to its native traditions of fantasy and metaphor and entered into a period of feverish avant-garde experimentation. Along with Beckett and Ionesco, Witkacy was discovered and given recognition as a precursor of the contemporary avant-garde theater.

He was more than a dead ancestor, he was a living creator. His plays were first performed by student theaters as part of the movement against the confines of socialist realism and censorship and for greater freedom of expression, and then, with the performance of *The Madman and the Nun* at the Narodowy Teatr in 1959, Witkacy started to be performed in the professional theaters, where he has now achieved the position of a modern classic. Without Witkacy, modern Polish avant-garde drama would simply not exist as we know it, nor would it have the importance and influence in the world that it enjoys today.

Another, although not final, stage in this unpredictable story came in July, 1967, with the production of *The Madman and the Nun* at the San Francisco State College Theater. After first stirring up some controversy on campus and fears of hostile community reaction to Walpurg's strange adventures, *The Madman and the Nun* proved to be tremendously successful with both the critics and the public. Almost three thousand spectators saw the play in four nights; only *West Side Story* has ever equaled its popularity in the history of our college theater.

This was the first production of Witkacy in America, or for that matter in the English language. It was directed by Jan Kott, who over thirty years ago as a young student sat in Witkiewicz' Warsaw apartment with the two shoemakers and the maid listening to Witkacy read *The Shoemakers*.

THE MADMAN AND THE NUN

The Madman and the Nun

INTRODUCTION

The Madman and the Nun (Wariat i zakonnica, 1923) serves as the best introduction to Witkiewicz' theater since it presents in compact form the major themes and techniques found in all his plays. Witkiewicz calls *The Madman and the Nun* a short play, and in performance it runs no more than ninety minutes. The cast is small, the single set a simple one: a bare cell for maniacs in a lunatic asylum. Brevity and condensation not only make *The Madman and the Nun* easy to perform, they also explain much of its impact. Restrictions give Witkiewicz a subject and a dramaturgical method. *The Madman and the Nun* contains charges of powder that are all the more explosive for being tightly packed. The madhouse is rocked by a chain of smaller blasts that finally set off the dazzling fireworks display of the final scene.

Witkiewicz makes confinement—and the resulting desire to break out of it—both the theme of his play and its form. The mad poet Walpurg (from Walpurgis Night in *Faust*) is confined in a cell in an insane asylum against his will and put into a straitjacket. Walpurg is looked after by psychiatrists in white uniforms and sisters in nuns' habits. The only window in the cell has twenty-five small, thick panes divided by metal bars; the door creaks on its heavy hinges each time it is unbolted and then bolted again. Walpurg is not allowed to write or do anything, except think endlessly. The tighter his confinement, the more intensely his mind works. Under the pressure of these physical restrictions, it seems to Walpurg that he is about to burst apart. Soon either he will break out, or his heart will burst.

Space on the stage becomes the total space in which all his life is lived. An intense struggle goes on in a small, enclosed area. Walpurg wants to be released from society's care and coercion in the name of benevolence, as well as from his own obsessions. He wants to escape imprisonment within the walls of society and of his own mind. Freedom is what he seeks, both from others and from himself. Even in his straitjacket, Walpurg constantly transcends the narrow space of his cell by his feverish reflections on art, poetry, and love. The juxtaposition of the imprisoned body and the mind roving far and wide generates dramatic tension.

The cell in the madhouse is also the cell of Walpurg's brain. We witness the workings of his mind as he struggles to break out of the mental straitjacket that has been put on him, both by society and by himself. Józef Szajna, the famous stage designer for the Warsaw production of *The Madman and the Nun* in 1959, describes how he made the cell into the interior of Walpurg's mind:

> The cell in Witkacy's *The Madman and the Nun* is represented by a wall that surrounds the hero of the play and the objects in the niches, a large moving head that spies on him, an automatic clock with the mechanism pulled out of it and the swaying symbol of unspecified biological form.
>
> The rocking lamp and the turned-up volume of the ticking of the clock are attuned to the mounting frenzy of the "madman's" monologue. They help define the emotion indirectly and by allusion. Acting on the principle of psychograms, the props penetrate to the levels that often escape direct and rational rules, increasing tension.[1]

In the 1967 production at San Francisco State College, Jan Kott used slide projections to penetrate into Walpurg's mind and Sister Anna's as well; clocks running backward and at different speeds created the sense of deranged time within the confines of the cell, cut off from all contact with normal life.

As well as transcending space, Walpurg ranges about in time, returning often to the past with a vision of an earlier stage of society, before science and technology existed, when an individual could rise above the common herd.

> Before, art wasn't perverted, there was no "insatiable craving for form." Life wasn't the aimless movement of soulless automatons. Society was not a machine. There was a soft, pulpy mass of suffering cattle, and out of it grew wonderful flowers of lust, power, creativeness, and cruelty.

A madman like Walpurg is still an individual and will not conform. Madness is a highly explosive, unpredictable force that cannot be controlled by abstract theories such as Grün's. Lust is another high explosive that can blow open the doors and windows of the asylum, and the introduction of Sister Anna, a deeply sensual woman who has become a nun only because of an unhappy love affair, sets off the dynamite already present in Walpurg. Deeply frustrated himself as a result of not seeing a woman for two years, the mad poet finds in Sister Anna an escape from himself, from his obsessions, and from his prison and his jailors. Sex is a creative and liberating force; Walpurg becomes Sister Anna's lover and starts to write again at the same time. However, as long as he is in the asylum, Walpurg is constantly being untied from his straitjacket and then tied up again by Sister Anna; his

---

[1] Józef Szajna, "Stuff the Stage Is Made Of," *Poland* (American Edition), No. 12 (December, 1965), p. 42.

enslavement is only interrupted from time to time by moments of secret freedom.

In *The Madman and the Nun* society is seen as not only a machine, but a machine with no one really in control. "Imagine a long row of machines in a huge factory without any engineer in charge. All the pointers on the dials have already gone beyond the red arrow, and everything rushes madly on." Those who have placed Walpurg in the asylum and are so sure of the distinction between sanity and madness are only cogs in the lunatic machine that first drives people mad and then locks them up. To Walpurg the whole world has been turned into a prison–lunatic asylum by figures of authority and power who crush life in the name of abstractions: science and religion. Dr. Grün and Sister Barbara are caricatures, grotesque puppets mouthing theories that break down in the face of the multiplicity of life. They are the absolute automationists who want to regiment life and lock up as lunatics those who think and feel differently from the way they do; theirs is a government by psychiatric dictatorship, declaring insane those who dare disagree with it.

The costumes indicate how Walpurg and Sister Anna have been confined; the straitjacket keeps Walpurg from writing and from embracing her, and Sister Anna's wimple and habit prevent her from responding to him until he has torn them off. The dramatic action develops by a series of disrobings and sudden violent outbursts releasing Walpurg from the confines of life as defined by the laws and regulations of the reigning scientific and religious establishment. Sister Anna first starts the process by untying his straitjacket; then Walpurg goes into his ascending spiral. He rips off Sister Anna's wimple and seduces her, kills Bidello with a pencil, threatens Grün with a penknife, breaks the windowpane and hangs himself with his straitjacket—a fitting revenge against the rational society that kept him alive benevolently so that he would not stop suffering prematurely.

But the play does not end there on a tragic note with the defeat of the mad poet at the hands of an evil society. Witkiewicz parodies such stereotypes. Even Walpurg and Anna are treated ironically. Walpurg is a parody *fin-de-siècle* poet who mocks his own calling and fatal passion and transcends his earthly sufferings. Enough forward motion and upward thrust have been generated by the early constrictions of space and time to catapult Walpurg into a world free of space and time—the world of his own dreams.

The last acts of Witkiewicz plays are often the strongest theatrically —the shortest, swiftest, and most startling, full of electrifying *coups de théâtre*. The volcano erupts. The imminence of revolution and the sudden explosive upheaval of subterranean forces—on both the personal and the social level—are axioms in Witkiewicz' analysis of man and society that make possible a maximum of unpredictability in the last half of his dramas, whereas in traditional dramaturgy the probabilities become more restricted as the play progresses, once certain premises have been established. In Witkiewicz, as in war and revolution, the longer the action goes on, the more the improbable and even the impossible become probable and possible.

In a state of insurrection, all the normal laws are suspended: anything can happen. The denouement of a normal play is the outcome of what has gone before and what the audience has been led to expect; in *The Madman and the Nun* the denouement is an insurrection against the whole established order—an insurrection against the laws of time, space, and motion, as well as against society and its rules. The uprising in *The Madman and the Nun* is against everything that has gone before; the denouement is not a consequence of what preceded it, but a refutation of it. Witkiewicz' *coups de théâtre* are like real *coups d'états*—they overthrow the preceding regime and undo a previous period of history.

Walpurg's return to life is a spectacularly comic *coup de théâtre*, exploding both the confines of the asylum and the expectations of the audience. His sudden re-entrance into the cell after he has hanged himself in everyone's presence is the opening blow of the revolution against the automated establishment. Its time-honored notions crumble; the earth begins to tremble for Grün and Sister Barbara—perhaps they are the ones who are insane.

Paradoxically, impossibly, yet appropriately, the mad poet and the debauched nun triumph and go into life and into town, escaping from the prison that man's science and religion have constructed. Dressed in new clothes, born anew, Walpurg and Sister Anna go free, liberated from morality and the laws of biology and physics. Time and space, which pressed so hard on Walpurg before, are totally extendable. The clock stops ticking in his head; he goes out the creaking door.

Arbitrary power is defeated by the revocation of the laws of matter; the victim escapes the victimizers, who are left to pummel one another and roll about on the floor with Walpurg's corpse, as he walks merrily out the door. The ending is a mock transcendental escape, a comic apotheosis; Walpurg's body is subject to all the laws of the physical world, but he himself transcends necessity as in a dream.

The rhythm of the play slowly mounts to this frenzied staccato. After the slow close-ups of Walpurg and Sister Anna in Act I, the action of the last two acts goes faster and faster, like the unattended machines described by Walpurg. In the final act all the movements are exaggerated; the characters hurl themselves about the stage and fling themselves at one another. Alfred and Paphnutius dash about the stage with the frantic, speeded-up rhythms and motions of the Keystone Cops.

The movements of the two attendants and Grün become more and more jerky and mechanical, as they succumb to the mechanistic theories in which they believe. They are the machine-driven, soulless automatons described by Walpurg at the beginning of the play. The victimizers become their own victims; they end up in a pulpy mass of struggling bodies, whereas Walpurg and Anna rise out of it, "wonderful flowers of lust, power, creativeness, and cruelty," like the fashionable yellow boutonniere in Walpurg's lapel. They are free.

Walpurg has fulfilled his earlier dream and gone back in time to a period when the artist was elegant, irresponsible, and free—above the groaning masses. The establishment, the madhouse managers themselves, go mad and sink back into primeval chaos in "the churning pulpy mass of bodies." "We're the madmen now. They've locked us up for good," one of the attendants cries out. The final grotesque fight between the psychiatrist and the Mother Superior and their minions is the result of their sudden discovery in themselves of all the insanity and aggression they had before tried to put onto Walpurg. A complete transfer has taken place: the mad are sane, and the sane are mad.

The Madman and the Nun

or, There Is Nothing Bad Which
Could Not Turn into Something Worse

**A SHORT PLAY IN
THREE ACTS AND FOUR SCENES**

Dedicated to all the madmen of the world

(y compris other planets of our system

and also planets of other suns in the Milky Way

and of other constellations)

and to Jan Mieczysławski

CHARACTERS

Alexander Walpurg	*29 years old. Dark-complexioned, very handsome, and perfectly built. Disheveled beard and mustache. Long hair. Dressed in a hospital gown. Straitjacket. Madman. Poet.*
Sister Anna	*22 years old. Very light blonde and very pretty, and to anyone who had "known" her, rather ardent. Fantastic nun's habit. A large cross on a chain on her chest.*
Sister Barbara	*Mother Superior. Dressed in the same costume as Sister Anna. 60 years old. A matron in the style of the Polish painter Matejko.*
Dr. Jan Bidello	*35 years old. Non-Freudian psychiatrist. Dark-complexioned with a beard. White uniform.*
Dr. Ephraim Grün	*Psychoanalyst of the Freudian school. A swarthy cherub in the Semitic style. White uniform.*
Professor Ernest Walldorff	*Jovial old boy, aged 55–60. Long white hair. Clean-shaven. Gold pince-nez. English sports jacket.*
Two Attendants	*Wild bearded beasts. Alfred—Bald, black beard. Paphnutius—Red hair and beard. Both dressed in hospital uniforms.*

The action takes place in a cell for raving maniacs in the lunatic asylum, At the Sign of the Jugged Hare.

ACT I

The stage represents a cell for raving maniacs. To the left there is a bed in the corner. Above the bed the inscription: Dementia Praecox, *Number 20. Opposite there is a window made up of twenty-five small, thick panes divided by metal bars. Under the window a table. One chair. To the right a door with creaking hinges. Alexander Walpurg is sleeping on the bed, tied in a straitjacket. A small light hangs from the ceiling. Dr. Bidello brings Sister Anna in.*

BIDELLO There's our patient. He's sleeping now after a large dose of chloral hydrate and morphine. Poison the hopeless cases slowly is our secret motto. However, perhaps Grün is right. I'm not one of those stubborn psychiatrists who are unwilling to accept anything new. I consent to this experiment, especially since Professor Walldorff and I have exhausted all other means. Dementia praecox. If you, Sister, could—although I very much doubt it—resolve the patient's "complex"—as the psychoanalysts call it—and penetrate, with the help of your feminine intuition, into the dark spot in his soul, the forgotten place, the "psychic wound," as they say, I would be only too delighted with Grün's success. As far as psychoanalysis is concerned, I acknowledge its diagnostic techniques, but have no confidence whatsoever in its therapeutic value. It is fine for those people who can devote their entire lives to being cured. Here's a chair. (*He offers her a chair.*)

SISTER ANNA Very well, Doctor, but what am I actually to do? How am I to go about it? I had almost forgotten to ask you the most important question.

BIDELLO Please don't attempt to do anything out of the ordinary, Sister. Behave quite naturally and directly, in accordance with your own intuition, as your conscience dictates. However, under no circumstances should you gratify his wishes. Do you understand, Sister?

SISTER ANNA Doctor, I should like to remind you that you are speaking to a member of a religious order.

BIDELLO Please don't be offended, Sister. A mere formality. Well, I'll say good-bye to you now. Something else: please remember that the most important thing is to bring to light his "complex," stemming from a forgotten incident in his past which has disturbed him ever since.

(*Sister Anna nods. Bidello leaves, bolting the door. Sister Anna sits down and prays. A pause. Walpurg wakes up and raises himself on the bed. Sister Anna trembles. She gets up and stands quite still.*)

WALPURG (*in a sitting position*) Is this a hallucination? This has never happened to me before. What's going on?

SISTER ANNA I am not a phantom. I have been sent to take care of you.

WALPURG (*getting up*) Aha. This is a new device on the part of my noble torturers.

> Devilish devices
> Impinge on our senses.
> But the soul lies concealed,
> No one wants it revealed.

What's your name? I haven't seen a woman for two years.

SISTER ANNA (*trembling*) My religious name is Anna.

WALPURG (*with sudden lust*) Well then, Sister, give me a sisterly kiss. Kiss me. I can't kiss you. You're so pretty. Oh! What agony! (*He draws nearer to her.*)

SISTER ANNA (*moving back, she speaks in a cold and distant tone of voice*) I am here to bring peace to your tortured soul. I, too, am beyond life. Don't you see my nun's habit?

WALPURG (*controlling himself*) Oh—I can't go on this way. I must control myself. (*In a different tone of voice*) Sister Anna, I'm a living corpse. I don't need help, only death.

SISTER ANNA I'm more dead than you. You will be cured, and then your whole life will lie before you. (*Walpurg gazes at her intently.*)

WALPURG Why are you a nun? You're so young, so beautiful.

SISTER ANNA Let's not talk about it.

WALPURG I must talk about it. You're very much like a woman who once was everything to me. Perhaps I'm only imagining it. She's not alive any more.

SISTER ANNA (*trembling*) Not alive?

WALPURG You, too, must have experienced something similar in your life. I felt it at once. He's not alive either, is he?

SISTER ANNA Oh, merciful God, let's not talk about that. I am now in a different world.

WALPURG But I am not. I envy you your other world; you've chosen your own home. But I have to live here, in this terrible prison, in a world my torturers have forced on me, in a world I hate. But my real world is this clock which is constantly ticking in my head—even while I'm asleep. I'd prefer death a thousand times. But I can't die. That is the decree for all of us madmen who suffer without being guilty. We're tortured as if we were the worst criminals. And we're not allowed to die because society is benevolent, so very benevolent that it doesn't want us to stop suffering prematurely. Ha! Please get me out of this damned straitjacket. I'm suffocating. My arms are pulling loose from their sockets.

SISTER ANNA I can't. The Doctor didn't give his permission.

WALPURG So you're in league with my executioners? All right! Sit down. Let's talk. We have time. Oh! I have so much time! Only I don't know what to do with it. And I can't stand my own thoughts—I can't stand—(*Stifling sobs*) . . . My thoughts go in circles, as if driven by a machine. There's an infernal machine going in my head. It's been set, but I don't know for what hour of what day. I don't know when it will go off. And I wait, I wait endlessly. At times I think that such torture cannot go on any longer. But no—a day passes, a night, another day, and then chloral hydrate, morphine, nightmares when I'm asleep, and that terrible sensation on waking up that everything is beginning all over again. And so on and on . . .

SISTER ANNA Please don't talk that way. Please, I beg you; calm yourself. If I can't help you at all I'll have to ask the doctor to relieve me of my duties here.

WALPURG (*wildly*) O no! You'll never get out of here! (*He controls himself; Sister Anna retreats in fear.*) Excuse me, Sister, I'm in full possession of my senses. Let's go on talking. I'll be calm now. Try to understand that I haven't seen a woman for two years . . . What were we talking about? Aha—you lost some one. So did I. Tell me about it. Please allow me to introduce myself. (*He bows.*) Walpurg. Alexander Walpurg.

SISTER ANNA (*reeling*) Walpurg? So it was your poetry my fiancé and I read together. Oh, how dreadful! And yet I'm grateful to you. How many beautiful moments I owe to you. And everything has ended so horribly.

WALPURG Perhaps because the two of you read my poetry together. And besides nothing has come to an end. The world goes on as if nothing has happened. But my third volume is not bad at all. I know what I'm talking about. After the third volume I decided to check into this hotel. Alcohol, morphine, cocaine—the end. And, to top it all, disaster.

SISTER ANNA How could you, with such talent! What happiness to be an artist like you!

WALPURG Happiness! Agony! I wanted to write myself out, to the very marrow, and die. But no. Society is benevolent. They saved me so that I could end my life being tortured here. Oh, their damn medical ethics! I'd like to murder that entire race of butchers. (*In a different tone*) Do you know, Sister, when I was in school, I studied Henrik von Kleist's biography. *"Er führte ein Leben voll Irrtum . . ."* I didn't understand it then. Now I understand it perfectly.

SISTER ANNA Why have you poisoned yourself with drugs? Tell me, please, I can't understand it at all. A genius like you.

WALPURG What? You don't understand? *"Meine Körperschale konnte nicht meine Geistesglut aushalten."* Who said that? My soul's fire has burned away my earthly shell. Now, don't you understand? My nerves weren't strong enough to resist that damnable something or other which compelled me to write. I had to poison myself. I had to gain strength. I didn't want to, but I had to. And once the whole machine, that old, weak machine starts its lunatic motion, it has to go further and further, whether I'm still creative or not. The mind's exhausted, but the machine goes on and on. That's why artists have to do insane things. What can you do with a senselessly accelerated motor which no one can control? Imagine a long row of machines in a huge factory without any engineer in charge. All the pointers on the dials have already gone beyond the red arrow, and everything rushes madly on.

SISTER ANNA (*listening with her arms crossed*) But why does it always end exactly like that nowadays? It used to be different.

WALPURG Before, art wasn't perverted, there was no "insatiable craving for form." Life wasn't the aimless movement of soulless automatons. Society was not a machine. There was a soft, pulpy mass of suffering cattle, and out of it grew wonderful flowers of lust, power, creativeness, and cruelty. But let's not pursue this conversation any further. Let's talk about life—about our life. I have as much compassion for you as you have for me.

SISTER ANNA My God, my God, my God . . .

WALPURG That's enough. There's only one thing certain: today the greatest art is found only in perversion and madness—I'm talking, of course, about form. But for the true creative artists, not the jackals, the forms they create are intimately connected to their lives. And now tell me about yourself, Sister. Who was he?

SISTER ANNA (*trembling and speaking mechanically*) He was an engineer.

WALPURG Ha, ha, ha, ha! And what happened?

SISTER ANNA (*offended*) Why are you laughing?

WALPURG I wasn't laughing at all. I only envy him. He was one of the small cogs in the machine, and not a demented pebble among meshed iron gears. Go on.

SISTER ANNA He loved only me, but he couldn't break off with a certain . . . woman. And finally he had to end it all. He blew out his brains. Then I entered the convent.

WALPURG What a lucky man! Don't feel sorry for him. So nowadays even engineers can have problems like that. And that's why you entered . . . Oh, how absurd. Why didn't I meet you first?

SISTER ANNA And what would have happened? You would have tortured me to death, the way you did that other woman . . .

WALPURG How do you know about that? Tell me this instant, how do you know that? No one knows anything about it. Who told you, Anna?

SISTER ANNA Please address me as Sister.

WALPURG (*quite coldly*) How does Sister know about it, then? That's interesting. I'm quite calm.

SISTER ANNA (*brutally*) Can't you understand? I'm talking to you, I know your poetry. I know who and what you are now.

WALPURG Oh, yes: I'm a madman in a straitjacket. It's that simple. But it isn't simple to torture someone to death the way I tortured her. I don't know which one of us killed the other. She sacrificed herself. In the final analysis I'm not guilty. She died of brain fever. I don't know if I killed her or if she is actually torturing me to death now—every day—systematically. After she died I read through her diary and then I understood with what dreadful, diabolical skill I had been tormenting her. But that's what she wanted. That's how she killed herself, and now she's killing me. Oh! (*He struggles in the straitjacket.*)

SISTER ANNA And how did you get in here?

WALPURG On account of my weak nervous system. Cocaine. The clock in my head. And that eternal question of whether I killed her or she killed me. Even in the fraction of a second I think two thoughts as different as God and Satan. What else is left? A few poems. They must have been published by now. My sister will make a little money from them. I have a sister whom I hate. What else is there? A little violence. And so I ended up here. But no one gets well here. You can see that for yourself. As a matter of fact I'm in full possession of my senses, I just happen to have a tiny machine in my head. Whoever comes here is finished. Because their type of cure only pushes you further and further into madness; you can try to tell them lies, but eventually you do something stupid, you make one false step, and then you're locked up forever.

SISTER ANNA Everything I've gone through seems so petty now. I used to believe that whatever happened to me was important and unique. Now there's nothing, only a terrible, hopeless emptiness. I don't exist now; he abandoned me forever.

WALPURG (*pleased*) He abandoned you, but only out of shame. For your sake he couldn't even give up some common slut, some demonic old bag, some obscenity or other. Yes, I'm sure. There's nothing at all important or unique in that. His death was proof of his despicable weakness. He couldn't do anything for you. But what about me? (*He falls on his knees before her.*) Please put your hand on my head. Perhaps the clock will stop ticking, at least for a moment. I'm composing poetry again now. But I think my poems are getting worse. I can't write any more. But then you can also use a pencil to kill yourself. I'll never improve, and yet new ideas come to me all the time. Sister, please hold my head in your hands. Oh, if only I could unscrew my head and put it away in a chest of drawers so that it could have a little rest. Then I could rest too.

SISTER ANNA Yes, yes, rest. Just a little. Like this. There. (*She takes his head in her hands and sinks into the chair. He puts his head on her knees.*)

WALPURG Untie my hands, would you? Really, I'm in full possession of my senses.

SISTER ANNA I can't. Please don't ask me to. The Doctor told me . . .

WALPURG (*without rising from his knees, he lifts his head up and looks at her wildly*) The Doctor? Do you want me to fly into a rage? It's always the same story here. You're their accomplice. First they drive you into a state of frenzy and then they put you in a straitjacket. And so it goes on endlessly. (*He pronounces these last words in a desperately hopeless way.*)

SISTER ANNA (*getting up*) Yes, yes . . . I know . . . Nothing else matters. I'll do anything for you. (*She lifts him up, turns him around so that his back is toward her, and unties the straitjacket. Walpurg turns around to face her and stretches out his arms, unrolling the sleeves of his straitjacket up to his elbows. He looks like a boxer getting ready for a fight.*)

WALPURG So—now I'm free.

SISTER ANNA (*fearfully*) Give me your word that nothing else will happen.

WALPURG Nothing else, only let's be happy even if it's only for a moment. You're the only woman in the world. Not because you simply happen to be the first woman I've seen for two years, but because you really are. When I'm with you, nothing else exists for me: my whole past, this prison, the tortures—it all disappears. I feel that I'll still write something more. Everything still lies before me. (*He draws quite near her.*)

SISTER ANNA (*not moving from where she is standing*) I'm afraid. It's all so horrible. Don't come any nearer.

WALPURG Do you think I'm going to hurt you? Do you think I'm going to humiliate you by forcing you to kiss me? I love you. You can trust me. I'm in full possession of my senses. (*He takes her hand. Sister Anna trembles as if she had touched red-hot iron.*) You are the only one. This moment, too, is the only one. It will never come back, nothing ever comes back. We live only once, and whatever is destined to happen on this earth must happen. Any other way, it's a crime which will poison future generations with its venom. Kiss me. What's your real name?

SISTER ANNA (*with no will of her own*) Alina.

WALPURG (*bringing his face close to hers*) Lina, I'm sure you love me. Don't imagine that I've always been this ugly. I didn't have a beard or mustache before. But once I tried to impale myself on the razor, and they stopped shaving me.

SISTER ANNA Oh—don't talk that way. I love you. Nothing exists in the whole world except you. Even eternal damnation . . .

WALPURG (*taking hold of her head in his hands and looking into her eyes*) There is no eternal damnation, the only rewards and punishments are right here in this world. Kiss me. I don't dare . . .

SISTER ANNA (*tearing herself away from him*) No, not that, not that! I'm afraid . . .

WALPURG (*tears off her wimple and clasps her in a wild embrace*) You must, you must. This moment is the only one . . . (*He kisses her on the lips, bending her backward. Sister Anna yields without any resistance.*)

ACT II

The same setting. Very early the next morning. It grows lighter and lighter, but the sky is overcast. A storm is approaching. Thunder and lightning become more and more intense.

SISTER ANNA (*putting on her wimple*) Now I have to tie you up again. How ghastly! But this is for you. I'm giving it to you as a talisman. (*She unfastens the iron cross from the chain she wears on her breast and gives it to him.*) I don't have the right to wear it any more. I had special permission from Mother Superior to wear it. My mother gave me this cross.

WALPURG Thank you, Lina. Thank you for everything. (*He takes the cross and puts it in a crevice in the slats of his bed.*) There was supposed to be a pencil and paper in there, but I never could find them. (*He comes back to her and kisses her hand.*) You know, it's only now that I realize how utterly miserable I've been—now that you love me. Yesterday simply to kiss your hair seemed beyond human happiness. Today, now that you're mine, nothing else matters. I want to get out of here, write, work, shave off my beard and mustache, dress well again. I want to live, to live a perfectly ordinary life. I must get out of here. You'll see. You've given me the strength to overcome anything. Let's both get out of here.

SISTER ANNA *(kissing him)* I feel exactly the same. I'm not a nun any more. I want to lead a normal, quiet life. I've gone through so much.

WALPURG *(gloomily)* Yes, of course, you'll get out. You're not in prison. *(With sudden anxiety)* Lina, don't betray me. That Doctor Bidello is my worst enemy. I prefer Grün, even though he's a disgusting pig, too. You won't betray me? I fear I've awakened your desires, and if you don't see me for a couple of days, someone else might begin to look attractive to you.

SISTER ANNA *(throwing her arms around his neck)* I love you. Only you forever and ever. I'd stay here myself if only you could get out. I love you for what you are. You must fulfill your destiny.

WALPURG Poor thing. I'm afraid for you. There's some violent force in me that I can't control. Necessity rules our lives. I have no will of my own, in the usual sense of the word. There's some higher power, above me or in me, whose orders I'm forced to follow.

SISTER ANNA That's creativity. Perhaps it's God. He will forgive us. And my mother will forgive us also, even though she was a saint.

WALPURG Wait just a minute, I haven't told you everything. It seems to me that maybe I did kill her. But you don't know . . .

SISTER ANNA *(tearing herself away from him)* Don't talk, don't say anything. Put this on quickly. They may come any minute. *(He stands with his back to her; she ties the sleeves of the straitjacket.)*

WALPURG But nothing's changed, has it? You're talking so strangely, as if you'd suddenly stopped loving me.

SISTER ANNA *(finishing tying him into the straitjacket)* Nothing's changed. It's just that I'm afraid. I fear for our happiness. *(She turns him toward her and kisses him quickly.)* And now lie down and pretend to be asleep. Hurry! *(She pushes him toward the bed.)*

WALPURG *(lying down)* Remember, don't betray me. There are so many attractive men in the world—so many scoundrels.

SISTER ANNA You're talking nonsense. Sssh! I think they're coming. *(Walpurg lies down and pretends to be asleep. Sister Anna sits down on the chair and prays. A pause. The door is unbolted and Dr. Bidello enters. Sister Barbara and Grün follow her.)*

GRÜN *(in the doorway, speaking to someone who is outside)* You can wait there. *(Bidello approaches Sister Anna and speaks with her in a low voice.)*

BIDELLO Well? How's it going? (*Sister Barbara kisses Sister Anna on the forehead, and Sister Anna kisses her hand.*)

SISTER ANNA All right. Everything is fine.

BIDELLO Has he been asleep the whole time? (*Grün listens attentively.*)

SISTER ANNA No. He woke up once. He talked quite coherently. He told me about his life. I didn't know that this is the famous Walpurg. Then he fell asleep peacefully. He didn't wake up a second time.

GRÜN Didn't I tell you so! He's beginning to resolve his complex. He fell asleep the second time without chloral hydrate. Has that ever happened in your experience, my dear colleague?

BIDELLO It's never happened to me at all. I never use chloral hydrate. But it's a curious phenomenon—the more so during a period of hysteria. Listen, Grün: I have no prejudices. If you want to try your methods further, go ahead. I consent. To tell the truth, I'm even beginning to believe in psychoanalysis. I'll turn my patient over to you. There's a little too much of the sexual in your theories. That's the only thing I still find questionable.

GRÜN But my dear colleague, the sexual drive is the most important thing in life. All complexes originate there. If you don't mind, I'll wake the patient up.

BIDELLO Go ahead. (*Bidello joins Sister Anna, and they move to stage right. Sister Barbara watches as Grün wakes Walpurg.*)

GRÜN (*waking Walpurg up*) Hello! Walpurg! Listen, it's me, Dr. Grün. (*Walpurg pretends that he is waking up. He stretches out on the bed and then sits up. A pause.*)

WALPURG Ah, it's you, Doctor. I haven't seen you for a long time. I enjoy our conversations together. Why don't you come more often? I suppose Bidello has forbidden you to?

GRÜN Nothing of the sort. He's entrusted you completely to my care. I'm certain that I can cure you. How did your conversation with Sister Anna affect you? That was my idea.

WALPURG It was miraculous. She's a saint. I never felt better in my whole life. I'd like to write again.

GRÜN Splendid. Today you will be given pencil and paper. Books too. What kind of books do you want?

WALPURG The complete works of Tadeusz Miciński and the second volume of Husserl's *Logische Untersuchungen*. Perhaps also Moréas. And the third volume of my own works. I feel so wonderful. Perhaps you'll be so kind as to introduce me to that tall lady dressed in a nun's habit. Duchess Vertigossa, I presume—if I'm not mistaken. (*He stands up.*)

SISTER BARBARA Mr. Walpurg, I am Sister Barbara, Mother Superior of the Convent of Voluntary Lady Martyrs. Please do not forget that.

GRÜN There's no need for me to introduce you if you two already know each other . . .

WALPURG Grün, perhaps you could take off my straitjacket? I'm stiff as a board, and besides, I'm in full possession of my senses now. I couldn't possibly have another attack of hysteria. I give you my word of honor. I slept like two tops . . .

BIDELLO (*breaking off his conversation with Sister Anna*) No, no, no! What's honor to a madman? No one knows. Hysteria when repressed breaks out every so often with redoubled strength. I can't give my consent. (*Walpurg controls a surge of hatred.*)

WALPURG But sir, Grün is willing to vouch for me with his life. Isn't that so, Grün?

GRÜN Yes. Listen, Bidello: it's either or—either he's my patient or he isn't. Halfway measures will get us nowhere.

BIDELLO Well, all right. Go to it. But what will Professor Walldorff say?

GRÜN In view of such good results, I'll answer for the Professor as well. Walpurg, I'll take off your straitjacket, and from now on I'm going to treat you as a convalescent. Turn around. (*Walpurg turns around so that he has his back to Grün. Grün unties the sleeves of his straitjacket.*)

SISTER BARBARA Isn't it somewhat premature, Dr. Grün?

GRÜN Sister Barbara, don't meddle in other people's business. If I were to analyze you, you'd leave the convent immediately. You have a penitence complex because of your guilt feelings toward your husband. Every minute he was alive, you tormented him in the most sadistic manner. I know everything.

SISTER BARBARA Do not forget yourself, Dr. Grün. Do not repeat vulgar town gossip in my presence.

GRÜN This isn't gossip. I know what the facts are. Walpurg, you're free. In six months we'll all leave here together and go into town. Look here, don't be so stubborn. Have confidence in me for once.

WALPURG (*shaking hands with him*) Thank you. (*To Sister Barbara*) At last I've found someone who can recognize a madman for what he is. I've had enough recognition as a poet. (*He shakes hands with Sister Barbara who looks at him disapprovingly.*) Grün, give me a pencil and a piece of paper. I must write down the first stanza of a new poem. The idea came to me in my sleep. I'll do wonderful things with it. (*Grün gives him a pad and pencil. Still standing, Walpurg begins to jot things down.*)

GRÜN (*to Sister Barbara*) You see, Sister, that's how one should treat the sick. Our hospitals are worse than medieval prisons. Only psychoanalysis will free mankind from the atrocious nightmare of the lunatic asylum. What I'm saying is that prisons would be empty if every one—from childhood on—were subjected to compulsory analysis which would eradicate all complexes. I can assure you that this man (*he points at Walpurg*) has a twin sister complex dating back to the time when he was still an embryo. That's why he cannot really fall in love. Subconsciously he loves his sister, although in his normal state of consciousness he feels genuine hatred for her. Walpurg, what's the first thing you associate with "sister"?

WALPURG (*crossing slowly to stage right*) Sinister—a cave—two orphans on a desert island—Vere Stacpoole's novel *Blue Lagoon*.

GRÜN Can you follow all that, Sister? The cave is the mother's womb. So is the desert island. I've resolved his complex. Now, on the second level, the novel—by the way, Sister, have you read it?—has penetrated into his already developed psychic placenta. Walpurg, in two weeks time you'll be fit as a fiddle.

WALPURG (*speaking to Bidello without paying attention to Grün*) Doctor, in my opinion it isn't right to flirt with a nun for quite such a long time.

SISTER ANNA (*Hurriedly*) We were only talking about you.

WALPURG What I told you was just between the two of us.

GRÜN (*to Sister Barbara*) You see, Sister, how rationally he's talking now? He's developing a healthy instinct for life. He's jealous—he can fall in love.

BIDELLO Really—at times I have to laugh at all this psychoanalytic nonsense. Ha, ha, ha! (*Walpurg seizes Bidello by the hair and gives him a terrible blow with his pencil on the left temple. Bidello falls to the ground without a groan.*)

WALPURG (*quietly*) That's for your flirtations with women in religious orders. (*He kicks Bidello with his foot.*) Croak, you filthy executioner! I'm only sorry I couldn't put him through a few tortures before he died. You see, that's a healthy instinct for life. Grün, lend me your penknife. My pencil is broken. That moron had a hard skull, but you don't have a rival any more.

SISTER ANNA (*who has been standing frozen with fear*) What have you done? It's all over now. (*She faints and falls to the ground.*)

GRÜN (*running up*) Walpurg, have you gone mad? I have a weak heart. O my God! Poor Bidello. (*He feels Bidello's pulse.*) He's dead —he hit him right in the temple.

WALPURG I'm completely cured now. First I identified him with my sister, and then I killed them both with one blow. I'm sure she died at that very moment. Ha, ha! My complex is resolved. If psychoanalysis is worth anything at all, I should be let out free at once. I'm not dangerous any more.

GRÜN Come now, Walpurg, aren't you making fun of me?

WALPURG No—I'm speaking quite seriously: I'm cured. That blow
to the skull cured me. That's why I'm not responsible for the murder, but from now on I will be responsible for everything I do in
the future. Mother Superior, you're in a daze—wake up; I was
simply defending the honor of a member of a religious order from
the advances of an ordinary Don Juan in a doctor's uniform. Isn't
that so? I'm sure this psycho-expert has had any number of love
affairs in the women's ward.

SISTER BARBARA These are untimely jokes. You are an utter madman.
And if not, you are an ordinary criminal. (*She goes to Sister Anna
and revives her.*)

GRÜN This is unheard of! So you really feel all right?

WALPURG (*impatiently*) I said so already, I'll consider my personal
enemy anyone who treats me like a madman. I'd like some breakfast
—I'm hungry. And please: look after Sister Anna. Can't you see that
she's not altogether well? The Duchess can't revive her.

GRÜN I can't believe it. He's resolved his complex all by himself, just as
easy as falling out of bed! It's quite incredible! (*He goes toward the
door.*)

SISTER ANNA (*coming to*) Oh! What will happen now?

SISTER BARBARA (*angrily*) Things will go on much the same as before.
We must not question the will of God. What have you done with
your cross?

SISTER ANNA Everything happened the way it did because today I left
my cross in the cell. My mother's cross was my only protection.

GRÜN (*shouting through the door*) Alfred! Paphnutius! Breakfast for
Number 20. (*The attendants appear.*)

SISTER BARBARA (*to Sister Anna*) You should be ashamed to believe in
such superstitions. Go at once to confession. (*The attendants come
in and are dumbfounded at the sight of Bidello's corpse.*)

SISTER ANNA Perhaps I'll go tomorrow. After what has happened, I am
unworthy. I must examine my conscience.

SISTER BARBARA (*pushing her toward the door*) Go this very minute!
Do you hear me?

WALPURG (*to Sister Anna*) Get a good rest, Sister, and come again this
evening. Our talks do wonders for me. After all, I couldn't talk
about myself with an idiot like Grün.

SISTER BARBARA (*turning around*) No—this must come to an end now.
I will not have my sisters turned into victims for murderers.

WALPURG Grün, your penknife.

GRÜN (*giving him the penknife without thinking*) But Sister Barbara, he will be tied up in his straitjacket, to be on the safe side. I can assure you there won't be any more crimes. (*To the attendants*) What are you blinking at? Bring his breakfast immediately. (*The attendants leave.*) He's almost completely cured. Jung describes a similar case. His patient became a model husband and an excellent architect after he butchered his aunt when she came to visit him. He had an aunt complex, and he resolved it. Psychoanalysis alone enabled him to do that.

SISTER ANNA (*not quite herself*) I am ready to sacrifice even my life, if that is necessary. Sister Barbara, I implore you, do not deny me penance for my grave sins.

SISTER BARBARA So be it—I consent. Perhaps God wills it. Perhaps in all of this there is some higher meaning not intelligible to us—the poor in spirit. Go to bed, Sister Anna, and do not go to confession today. And this evening you will come on duty at ten o'clock. (*Both of them leave, passing the attendants who are bringing in breakfast. Walpurg has sharpened his pencil and is writing.*)

GRÜN Eat, Walpurg. You deserve a decent meal after all this. As a psychoanalyst I understand and forgive everything. There is no crime without a complex, and a complex is a sickness.

WALPURG Just a moment—don't interrupt me. The last line . . . I need one more word . . . (*He writes.*)

GRÜN (*to the attendants*) Why are you just standing there, you blockheads? Take the Doctor's body to Section 7. (*The attendants take up Bidello's corpse and leave.*)

WALPURG There, I've finished. Now I've finally cleared my brain of the last trace of madness. The clock has stopped ticking. I have no pangs of conscience whatsoever. (*He attacks his breakfast with enthusiasm. The storm is gathering momentum. Green shafts of lightning intermittently pierce the dark gray shadows. Rain beats against the window.*)

GRÜN A wonderful lesson for the old psychiatric school. I'll write a monograph about you. I'll be world famous.

WALPURG (*sitting and eating with a hearty appetite*) Psychiatry received its best lesson in the person of Mr. Bidello. I never liked that idiot or his manners toward women. I've known him for a long time. For the last five years he saw me as a victim. But when he began to interrelate with sister, then I couldn't stand it any longer. Ha, ha, ha!

GRÜN (*rushes to Walpurg and gives him a hug*) Walpurg! You're the greatest genius in the world! I love you. Together we've created something wonderful.

WALPURG (*suddenly stands up and pushes Grün away. Grün*

staggers.) Enough of your familiarity! Don't pester me! Idiot! He's grown as familiar with me as he would with any of his psychiatric cases. Keep your distance! Do you understand?

GRÜN (*jumping back*) Give me back my penknife! Give me back my penknife!

WALPURG (*throws the penknife on the floor for him; Grün picks it up*) There you are, you coward! One murder per day is quite enough for me. It isn't my custom to trample on cockroaches. Get out!

GRÜN (*retreating toward the door, he opens the penknife*) Paphnutius! Alfred! (*The attendants rush in.*) Put Number 20 in his straitjacket! Quickly! (*With phenomenal speed the attendants throw themselves upon Walpurg, put him in the straitjacket, and tie the sleeves. Walpurg doesn't resist at all.*)

WALPURG Ha, ha, ha, ha! A game of make-believe. We madmen are the shrewdest people. Our instincts are so wonderfully acute that even animals seem stupid in comparison.

GRÜN (*closing his penknife*) Laugh, Walpurg, laugh. No matter what you do, you'll be cured. I'm not interested in you or your silly versifying. The only important thing is that "dementia praecox," as it is called, can in fact be cured by resolving complexes. Let's go. (*He goes toward the door, and the attendants follow him.*)

ACT III

The same setting. The light which hangs from the ceiling is burning. Sister Anna unties Walpurg's straitjacket.

SISTER ANNA You must be very tired, my poor dear.

WALPURG Not at all, not at all. I slept like a log all day long. I slept away fifteen years of sleeplessness. I feel splendid. (*Sister Anna takes off his straitjacket. He turns around and faces her.*) And do you actually know, after all that's happened, I think there's no place on earth worthy of me except this cell. I don't even have any desire to leave it. Read my poem. I have stage fright—I can't.

SISTER ANNA (*reading*) Oh—it's absolutely marvelous!

> I am reading the Bible under a tree, and time is fleeting,
> Narcotics lurk among the shrubs covered with sun, dew, and flowers,
> In the midst of the breath of the morning breeze,
> Give me milk—milk straight from the cow,
> And eggs—straight from the hen;

I want to be healthy, one of the good guys,
I want to hold my head up high.
But suddenly the simple question: "What for? Is it worth it?"—
And mouth wide open
I've sucked in every drug at once,
And pale as paper, sheet, or handkerchief
I've plunged into the whirlpool of an unknown battle with an un-
   known foe
Who may be Satan, who may be God.
This is no battle
Only: "Draw in the reins! Ready arms! March!"
Only: the stuffing of my brains rammed into other men's skulls.
Superb! But when you're with me, everything will be different. Isn't
that so? No more drugs. I'll be everything to you.

WALPURG Perhaps so. But first of all—come what may—we must get
out of here as soon as possible. Only don't go into excessive ecstasies
over my works. This is the beginning of something entirely new,
but in itself it's nothing.

SISTER ANNA (*sitting down beside him*) You know—I'm so happy I
feel guilty. Oh—if only I could suffer a little. Life beyond this cell
has no meaning for me either. If we were left here for all eternity, I
would be perfectly satisfied. It's so absolutely marvelous to be with
you. Everything has meaning now. And to think that I lived a
completely senseless life for so long! Darling, I must confess when
you killed Bidello, you aroused my desires to the point of madness.
You excite me tremendously! It's monstrous.

WALPURG (*embracing her with sudden lust*) My perverse darling! (*In
a different tone*) If only I were allowed to write when I'm here
alone! I must keep myself completely in check so that that nitwit
won't have me put back in the straitjacket. Yesterday I couldn't
control my emotions: I had to kill that hideous brute.

SISTER ANNA Don't talk about it, Alex. Rest. Lean against me, and let's
forget all that. I'd like to make up for those two agonizing years
you've gone through. We have no idea what awaits us.

WALPURG Everything will be all right now. We'll go somewhere far
away, as far as the tropics. I was there once with her. In Ceylon. But
her ghost won't disturb us now. That was madness, the same as your
love for your idiot. We are destined for each other. We're that ideal
couple whose meeting the universe demanded. Oh—why didn't it
happen sooner!

SISTER ANNA But perhaps it's better this way? Otherwise we never
would have been able to understand each other.

WALPURG Let me kiss you. I love you. You and you alone are an

intimate part of me and of what I have to write. For you I can create
things I never could have expressed at all without your love.

SISTER ANNA My one and only . . . (*They kiss for a long time, more
and more passionately. There is a sudden click of the door being
unbolted, and in rush Grün, the two attendants, and Sister Barbara.
Walpurg and Sister Anna jump up.*)

WALPURG Too late! (*He stands with his arms crossed on his chest.
Sister Anna sits frozen with fear and shame.*)

GRÜN Ha, ha! Too early, rather. So that's how it is, is it, my good
Sister! So that's the secret of your successful treatment of my
patient. (*They all stand in such a way that Grün is nearest Walpurg
and Sister Anna; Sister Barbara is farther away, and the two attendants are still farther away. They make a row parallel to the foot-
lights.*) The late Bidello was right after all. (*Sister Anna throws
herself toward Grün, but faints and falls.*) But psychoanalysis can
cope even with this.

SISTER BARBARA This is horrible! A criminal and a wanton in a nun's
habit! This will be my death blow. (*She covers her eyes with both
hands.*)

GRÜN (*to the attendants*) Put him in the straitjacket! I'll show him! He
concealed from me a complex I didn't know about. And he pre-
tended that he had a sister complex. But there must be repressed
truth even in lies. That's Freud's fundamental position. (*The attendants throw themselves at Walpurg.*)

WALPURG (*in a ghastly voice*) Everyone stay where he is! Not one
step! (*Startled by his screaming, they all come to a standstill in rigid
poses and "freeze." With frantic speed Walpurg pulls the cross out
of the crevice in the bed and shouts*) Now I'll show you something,
you psychic murderers! (*As if hypnotized, all the others remain
frozen in the furtive and stealthy movements they were making.*)
Scum! (*He jumps up on the table, knocks out two sections of the
window with the cross, and ties one sleeve of his straitjacket to the
bar between them. He ties the other sleeve around his neck and
stands up on the table, facing the audience with his arms spread out
like a cross, bending forward with a gesture as if he were going to
throw himself down.*) And now see what is going to happen, and
may my blood be on you! (*He starts to throw himself down.*)

Scene 2, without any intermission

*While the curtain is down (which should be as short a time as
possible), the actor playing Walpurg unties himself and goes off
quickly to the dressing room, and stagehands tie to the sleeve of his*

*straitjacket a dummy which closely resembles Walpurg (a good sculp-
tor must make the mask), but in a hanged condition. When the curtain
goes up, everybody on stage should stand in the same positions as in
Scene 1. All of this lasts only a moment (1–2 seconds).*

GRÜN *(throwing himself toward Walpurg's corpse)* Cut him down!
   *(The attendants rush forward and take down Walpurg's corpse
   from the sleeve of the straightjacket. Grün examines him. Sister
   Anna jumps up.)*

SISTER ANNA What has happened?

SISTER BARBARA Your lover has hanged himself, you shameless creature!
   That's what has happened! May God forgive you . . . I cannot. I'm
   going to lock you up for your entire life. You'll rot in a dungeon
   . . . You . . . *(She chokes with rage and indignation.)*

SISTER ANNA Oh! Oh! Oh! *(In a sudden rage)* All of you killed
   him—you criminals! *(She throws herself upon the corpse.)*

GRÜN *(getting up)* Dead. His spine is broken. The epistropheus has
   penetrated the medulla oblongata. We've lost our guinea pig. The
   question is: did he die a sick man, or was this, so to speak, the final
   action of a sick man whereby he would have become cured? Or
   perhaps he hanged himself already cured? That would be dreadful!

SISTER ANNA *(by the corpse)* Save him instead of spouting nonsense!
   He's still warm.

GRÜN I said he's dead. You don't know anything about anatomy. His
   breathing has stopped. Not even psychoanalysis can help him now.
   But what has he got in his hand? What did he knock out the pane of
   glass with? I completely forgot about that problem. *(He approaches
   the corpse.)*

SISTER ANNA *(she wrenches the cross out of the corpse's clenched
   fist)* It's mine! I won't give it to you! I gave it to him as a talisman!

GRÜN Give it to me this very minute, Sister. *(He grabs the cross out of
   her hand.)* A cross. The one she always wore on her breast. *(He
   turns to Sister Barbara.)*

SISTER BARBARA Yet another sacrilege. *Quelque chose d'énorme!* It's her
   mother's cross, which I allowed her to wear as a favor in view of her
   irreproachable conduct. *(Sister Anna gets up and, staggering as if
   she were drunk, approaches Sister Barbara.)*

SISTER ANNA I beseech you! Forgiveness! I shall die in despair. I have
   nothing at all now: not even the possibility of penance. *(She falls on
   her knees before Sister Barbara.)*

SISTER BARBARA Your place is in the streets! Slut! Oh, *quelle salope!*
   Away from me! *(Still on her knees, Sister Anna lowers her face to
   the floor and freezes in that position. Her hands sink spasmodically*

into her crumpled headdress. Sister Barbara kneels down and prays.)

GRÜN Well—Alfred! Paphnutius! Take corpse Number 20 to the dis-
secting room. That idiot Professor Walldorff will undoubtedly want
to perform an autopsy and look for brain damage. Ha, ha! Let him
look! (*Meanwhile the attendants pick up Walpurg's body and start
to carry it toward the door. To Sister Anna*) Well—Sister Anna,
pull yourself together and let's get out of here at long last.

(*At this moment the door opens and Walpurg comes in. He is
clean-shaven, mustache y compris. His hair has been trimmed. He
is dressed in an impeccably tailored cutaway coat. He wears a
yellow flower in his lapel. Bidello, dressed in a black frock coat,
comes in after him. On his arm he is carrying a woman's dress in
dark colors, blue and violet, and also a woman's hat. Professor
Walldorff can be seen behind him.*)

WALPURG Lina! Get up! It's me, Alex.

(*They are all dumbfounded. Sister Barbara springs up off her
knees. Grün stares at Walpurg with his mouth open and is not able
to catch his breath. The attendants drop Walpurg's body which, in
the stillness of the room, crashes to the ground with a bang. Sister
Anna springs up and looks at Walpurg speechlessly.*)

SISTER ANNA (*throwing herself at Walpurg*) Darling! Is it really you?
And what's that? (*She points at the corpse.*) Oh—what does it
matter, I'm so happy I'll probably go mad. You're so attractive! My
one and only! (*She falls into his arms. They kiss.*)

BIDELLO We're going into town. Oh—here's a dress for you, Miss
Alina, and a hat. Alexander and I picked these things out in a hurry.
At first glance. You'll have to change your clothes. Perhaps these
will do for the time being.

WALPURG Let's go. I'm really completely sane now: sane and happy. I'll
write something marvelous. (*He leads Alina out. Bidello follows
them.*)

BIDELLO Keep well, Grün. And after this, analyze yourself thoroughly.
(*He leaves. Professor Walldorff sticks his head in the door.*)

WALLDORFF Well, ladies and gentlemen? Hee, hee, hee!

GRÜN (*his lips blanched*) Pro-fess-or . . . I . . . I don't know . . .
(*Suddenly he begins to shout in a terrible voice.*) I don't know what
the hell is going on here! (*He approaches the door slowly, clutching
his head in his hands. Sister Barbara stares straight ahead, fiercely and
madly. The attendants look alternatingly at the corpse and at Walldorff.*)

WALLDORFF Oh, it doesn't matter. I'm through with psychiatry. I'm
going back to surgery. Brain operations once made me famous. And
I am taking Bidello as my assist——

GRÜN (*throwing himself toward him*) Aaaaa! That's blackmail!

WALLDORFF Oh no! (*Pushing him away*) Hop! Skip! And away! (*He shuts the door and bolts it from the outside. Grün stands helplessly and stares wildly about at the others.*)

GRÜN Now—oh—suddenly I feel a new complex coming on. But what kind of a complex? (*He screams.*) I don't know what any of this is all about! (*The attendants suddenly spring away from the corpse and, roaring with terror, fling themselves at the door and feverishly attempt to open it.*)

SISTER BARBARA (*in a state of wild despair*) That's all your psychiatry is! (*Sobbing*) In my declining years I cannot tell any more who is mad—you or I or those people. Oh, my God, my God! Take pity on me. Perhaps I've already gone mad. (*She falls on her knees, stretching out her hands to heaven.*)

ALFRED We're the madmen now. They've locked us up for good. And this guy here, he's still lying there right in front of us, but that same Number 20 without the beard, he got up and went out there.

PAPHNUTIUS (*pointing at Grün*) He's the one—he's the worst madman. Hit him, Fred! Give it to him! Harder! Till you can't lift your arm any more!

GRÜN Stay where you are! I can explain it all to you. Perhaps at the same time it will become clearer to me too.

PAPHNUTIUS Explain it to yourself if you're so smart. Take that!

(*He starts to beat him. Alfred throws himself at Grün also, and they both thrash him. In order to save Grün, Sister Barbara throws herself forward and becomes intertwined with the fighters. There arises a so-called "obshchaya roukopashnaya schvatka à la manière russe" [a rough-and-tumble, hand-to-hand free-for-all in the Russian manner], reminiscent of so-called "samosoude" [mob law]. All four of them roll on the floor, hitting one another right and left. Walpurg's corpse becomes absorbed into this heap of thrashing bodies, and it rolls about among them passively. Blinding blue light, from above, fills the stage. Other overhead lamps are turned off, and in a bright elliptical circle of light the only thing visible is the churning pulpy mass of bodies. The curtain drops slowly.*)

7 January 1923

The artist-painter Iwo Gall devised an absolutely diabolic scheme for the scenery for this play. Anyone planning to produce the play should get in touch with him. This is the author's formal stipulation: otherwise nothing doing. [Author's note]

The Water Hen

INTRODUCTION

The Water Hen (*Kurka Wodna*), written in 1921, was performed once during Witkiewicz' lifetime, at the Słowacki Theater in Cracow in July, 1922. The critics were hostile, and Witkiewicz responded with one of his typical polemic defenses of his own theories in an essay called "Some Unessential Remarks about *The Water Hen*." First he denies that the play is in any way autobiographical, as had been suggested by a friend during the intermission of the first performance. Then the playwright predicts his own vindication as an artist in ages to come:

> It's possible not to like me as an artist, but to say that I'm not an artist at all I consider something of an exaggeration, and I'm afraid that the judgment of future generations about some of my critics will not be particularly flattering.

Although he was not totally satisfied with the production because of the inadequate sets, Witkiewicz holds up *The Water Hen* as a good example of Pure Form in the theater. Along with the Epilogue to *The Mother*, *The Water Hen* in its entirety serves as the best illustration of Witkiewicz' theory. When the play is seen as Pure Form, the feeling of bewilderment it arouses in the audience can be accepted as the new theatrical effect the playwright is aiming for and understood and appreciated as such.

At the beginning of Act II of *The Water Hen*, the Duchess of Nevermore cautions her precocious stepson Tadzio: "No one knows why things are the way they are and not some other way. You can ask such questions endlessly and never find any answers." Like Tadzio, we are endlessly trapped into asking unanswerable and possibly irrelevant questions. Why is the Water Hen a water hen? Where does Tadzio come from? Who is the Lamplighter? Is Edgar Tadzio's father? Or is he really Edgar Nevermore? What does any of it mean? Witkiewicz' art lies in the creation of a feeling that there are questions without answers. The play confronts us with another world—a world of strange dreams and unfathomable mysteries—which compels us to wonder why things are the way they are and not some other way.

This metaphysical feeling of wonder and stupefaction is precisely what Witkiewicz argues the theater should create in the spectator. The new type of play Witkiewicz proposes in *An Introduction to the Theory of Pure Form in the Theater* will imitate not real life, but the pure arts of painting and music. Unhampered by such obsolete notions as believable characters and consistent plots, the dramatist will be free to deform reality for purely formal ends and use all the elements of theater as the musician uses notes and the modern painter colors and shapes. The spectator will be transported into a new dimension of thought and feeling, a world of "nonsensicality" where everything is free and unpredictable. *The Water Hen* seems to fit admirably Witkiewicz' suggestion that the new type of play is like "some strange dream, in which even the most ordinary things had a strange, unfathomable charm, characteristic of dream reveries, and unlike anything else in the world."

According to Witkiewicz' own theory, it might seem futile to try to discuss the meaning of *The Water Hen,* rather than simply to admire its brilliant design. After all, we do not ask what Bach's *Chromatic Fantasy and Fugue* means. However, the structure of each is explicable; internal construction, not subject matter, discloses the formal meaning of such art. If it is impossible to say why eight concentric rays of intense green light fill the stage when the Lamplighter appears after Edgar kills the Water Hen, at least it is clear that his reappearance in Act III takes us back in time and place to the beginning of Act I. His octagonal lantern lights the way for Edgar to shoot the Water Hen again. These sudden changes in perspective are part of a formal pattern of recurrence and inversion, giving the play both a pictorial and a musical quality.

Yet beneath its beauty as mystification and formal exercise, its brilliant surface, we begin to detect shapes and reflections if we peer long enough into its depths. Since human beings are the chief elements in drama, Witkiewicz maintained that theater can never be perfectly abstract like the pure arts of painting and music. Even though each element from real life is used only as a splash of color in the composition, *The Water Hen* paints man against the background of the universe, state, society, revolution, time, sex, money, art. The form may be pure, but the materials are the impure facts of life in the twentieth century.

So, if *The Water Hen* asserts nothing, it still says something about a strange world, which is not our world, but which resembles it seen from a great distance. In this "spherical tragedy," man sees himself as the universe sees him. It is a nonhuman drama about humans: "People are like insects, and Infinity surrounds them and summons them in a mysterious voice." The Witkacian world is little and lost in the cosmos. "Our small globe" the Duchess of Nevermore calls it—it is only one among many possible worlds, creations, planets, stars, spheres rolling and spinning in the void. Man is alone, forced at each moment to create himself and his world: every morning Edgar must start the day from scratch. On a new and unfamiliar shore each character has to create a life (or lives) for himself. Witkiewicz sees Robinson Crusoe and his desert island everywhere.

The Water Hen is a play about creation. The Father is a creator, trying to make an artist out of his son. Tadzio wants to create a mother and father, but he is at home nowhere; even the accordion-playing gangster Korbowski has equal rights at Nevermore Palace. Edgar labors to invent some sort of life for himself: "I should have been somebody, but I never knew what, or rather who." He is not even sure if he exists until he can climb inside other people's lives. "My friend's wife—my mistress' son. At last I've created a family for myself!"

Edgar even has to create his own fake penance and suffering with the aid of an obsolete torture machine from the Nevermore museum. In this world, everything—above all, human emotion—is synthetic and secondhand. Edgar looks back to the past for scraps to hold on to: a costume, a phrase, a murder, someone else's wife and son. He has no future, no present; he is nothing and has nothing, except scraps. He is a ham with a few fake grandiloquent gestures and phrases from the past —but with no identity. Even at Nevermore Palace he is only a transient lodger, a fraudulent hero in a sham world.

Tadzio has had enough and accuses his elders of too much creativity: "Manufacturing artificial people, artificial crimes, artificial penance, artificial everything." The play abounds in unnatural concoctions. The Water Hen fed the ginger cat lemons. The Duchess and the Three Old Men—the aristocracy and the money interests—create an incongruous amalgam of classes and races in the Theosophical Jam Company, blending the spiritual and the material in a sticky mixture. The names of the characters—Ephemer Typowicz (an ephemeral type), Specter, Evader—indicate that the speculation is risky and the boom will not last.

New groupings, hybrid graftings, preposterous fusions—the play's motion is generated by the odd malleability and mutability of matter. At the end of the play, an uprising occurs, a new revolutionary society is in the process of creation, as makeshift, insubstantial, and inauthentic as Edgar's calling, marriage, and paternity. Manikins and marionettes: this is the second Genesis of trash and dummies, parodies of true creation. In The Street of Crocodiles (1934), Bruno Schulz gives the Father the views of his friend and mentor Witkiewicz: [1]

[1] Henryk Bereza, "Bruno Schulz," Polish Perspectives, IX, No. 6 (June, 1965), 37–39.

Demiurge was in love with consummate, superb and complicated materials; we shall give priority to trash. We are simply entranced and enchanted by the cheapness, shabbiness and inferiority of material. . . . Can you imagine the pain, the dull imprisoned suffering, hewn into the matter of that dummy which does not know why it must be what it is, why it must remain in that forcibly imposed form which is no more than a parody? [2]

Parody and improvisation are Witkiewicz' weapons in devising a cosmogony of trash and a metaphysics for manikins. Compared to those two older birds, *The Wild Duck* and *The Seagull*, with their ornate symbolic plumage, *The Water Hen* is a wooden decoy. In "Some Unessential Remarks" Witkiewicz explained: "Unquestionably there is some kind of analogous meaning to the words Water Hen and Wild Duck—both signify birds. But what else there might be in common with Ibsen's play I really could not say."

Witkiewicz' plays often start as gags parodying drama in the older style of creation; titles, characters, and situations from other works kindle his imagination, and he experiments deforming them and pushing them into a new dimension. For a willfully distorted view of an ersatz world, clowning and pranks are indispensable. The names of his characters often contain ingenious private jokes: the Water Hen (*Kurka Wodna*) is a secret anagram for an obscene word for whore (*kurwa*). Sometimes the names are international literary parodies in foreign languages. Instead of being the refrain of Poe's Raven, Witkiewicz makes the Nevermores into characters and continues his bird lore. Like his frequent garbled quotations, misattributions, and invented citations, Witkiewicz' playing with names and titles is a purposeful prank in Pure Form. Everything is haphazard and chaotic and turns into something else: "Art, philosophy, love, science, society—one huge mishmash," in the words of the hero of *The Cuttlefish*.

"A Spherical Tragedy" is the subtitle of *The Water Hen*. All points on its surface are equidistant from its center. Like our small globe, it has no beginning, middle, or end; its structure is circular, finishing where it began with the shooting of the Water Hen. Such a sphere is a separate world, whirling about in space. Witkiewicz brings drama into the world of modern physics and mathematics (as well as of modern painting). The Hungarian mathematician János Bolyai, author of the *Science of Absolute Space*, wrote to his mathematician father: "*from nothing I have created another wholly new world!*" So another son to another father about his new creation. Witkiewicz calls one of his plays written at just this time a "non-Euclidean drama." *The Water Hen*

[2] Bruno Schulz, *The Street of Crocodiles*, translated by Celina Wieniewska (New York: Walker and Company, 1963), pp. 51, 54.

likewise rejects classical geometry for the spherical variety in which the shortest distance between two points is a curve, and parallel lines always meet.

The play moves from zero to infinity, both of which are spherical. Edgar is nothing, a void everyone tries to fill. Tadzio discovers Infinity after Edgar has killed the Water Hen—and she claims she does not exist at all. Spheres and numbers: the construction of artificial worlds. The Duchess' former husband Edgar was reading Russell and Whitehead's *Principia Mathematica* after his entrails had been devoured by a tiger in the Janjapara Jungle. At the beginning of Act II, Tadzio is putting together some kind of mechanical device, and after he has grown up, he studies mathematics. In Witkiewicz, figures and machines start to replace life; the world will soon become totally automatic. The card game (vint in the original) at the end of the play is another construction, paralleling, with its astronomical scores, the heaps of corpses in the streets and all the confiscated property. Matter is endlessly pliable. Even Korbowski rolls up into a ball and becomes a world.

But it is all lies—everything men say and do and all the roles they invent. "Truth is what is actually happening," according to the Water Hen. Suddenly the scene changes: two walls are slid in from the sides, and the field becomes the courtyard of a barracks; or the cherry-colored curtain is drawn, and the landscape with pole and lighted lantern appears between the columns. A rapid shift in perspective, a lifting of the veil, the painted scene is pulled apart, and something strange appears behind it. The colored fragments in the kaleidoscope are shaken; we look through to the view cards of revolution in the background.

The exotic world of international finance, sex, art, and politics—crossroads of different races and peoples—finally blows up. The social spheres—duchesses, artists, sea captains, detectives, crooks, and Russian nannies—are spinning out of control too. Edgar's father will turn into a revolutionary admiral; Edgar and the Water Hen have been transformed into corpses, along with the others in the streets. *The Water Hen* is not only a "spherical tragedy," it is also a "comedy with corpses," another genre invented by Witkiewicz.

It is an a-realistic world, an animated still life of ginger cats and lemons. The outbreak of revolution is no more or less surprising than anything else, and the corpses, "the really frightful things," Witkiewicz, like Tadzio, paints only through a prism of vivid color. The red glare of exploding shells lights the whites and grays and blacks of the mustaches, beards, and hair of the four elderly gentlemen playing cards during the revolution. They are playing-cards themselves—kings and jacks. The bombs are their lantern.

The Water Hen is the painting of a collective dream, a playful excursion into a new dimension of cataclysmic science fiction. It is impossible to do anything with such a society—life cannot become any more artificial, automatic, and false. Here is a cardboard universe for which there is no bid, simply "Pass."

Despite Witkiewicz' strictures, Pure Form cannot explain all of *The Water Hen*, especially not its strong emotional force and its richness as a personal, social, and political statement. It is a family tragedy, dealing with "three abortive generations" and two sets of fathers and sons; their refined, anguished world is on the brink of disaster, and they face emotional and social bankruptcy. From this perspective, *The Water Hen* is surrealistic Chekhov, a fantastic *Cherry Orchard* with gangsters. Instead of the mysterious sound of a harp string snapping and the chopping down of the cherry trees, the rattle of machine guns punctuates the collapse of Witkiewicz' vanishing world.

Like Chekhov, Witkiewicz portrays with poignancy and humor in the first two acts of *The Water Hen* the leisurely life of the upper class on a country estate, attended by servants and consumed by a sense of futility and boredom that is only temporarily relieved by pointless love affairs. As in Chekhov, too, there is a considerable interval of time elapsing between the next to last act and the last act so as to permit the initial situation to deteriorate. However, Witkiewicz deliberately pushes this technique to extremes. Whereas in Chekhov there is simply a gradual and deepening sense of frustration, regret, and futility after the passage of several months, in *The Water Hen* ten years elapse suddenly. In a startling parody of stage servants conveying necessary information to the audience, the Footman announces to Tadzio: "Sir, the Lady who was here ten years ago wishes to speak to you." The changes that have resulted are drastic; the world and the people in it have grown hard, violent, and sick.

The enigmatic Hen who was once so close to Edgar has become a coarse and unscrupulous seductress sticking her claws into Tadzio. Edgar has aged prematurely, and his dissatisfaction with life and search for identity have turned to a hopeless despair driving him to suicide. Tadzio has gone from a dreamy and precocious child, deeply devoted to the father who adopted him, to a brash, bitter young man who hates Edgar and chooses Korbowski as his ideal. Korbowski himself has ceased to be simply the ridiculous k'pt man paid by the Duchess and has become a hardened criminal and ruthless opportunist. The rhythm of life has utterly changed. Mid-twentieth-century nervousness and tension have replaced the old leisurely ennui; Tadzio's schedule is so busy that he even forgets that women exist, and Edgar has been thrown into the business world: "board meetings at banks, the stock exchange, negotiations with wholesalers and big accounts." The new science is mathematics, and the new world no longer has time for amorous or metaphysical pursuits. Family relations degenerate into a bitter struggle between the new father and new son, Edgar and Tadzio, ending with a physical fight between the two. The decay of the bonds of personal relationships has gone so far that the collapse of society in revolution seems surprisingly convincing, even though it has never been hinted at. Witkiewicz has a Shakespearean grasp on the interrelationship between public and private disaster; when father and son come to blows, it is symptomatic of violence on a broad scale.

The old sea captain is the only character who does not change. His boundless optimism and lack of neurosis make him at first seem the only sane person in a crowd of madmen; his humor and bluntness cast him in a role of a comic chorus, particularly when he talks of his favorite subject, his son's artistic vocation. But, in the last act, his heartiness and lack of concern in the face of disasters that overtake his son and family are a frightening kind of moral insensitivity or something worse. His failure to change or stop joking and his assurance that he will become a "revolutionary admiral" are cynical examples of the power of the human animal to survive. The more sensitive go under.

The Water Hen

A SPHERICAL TRAGEDY
IN THREE ACTS

Father	*Albert Valpor, an old man, former skipper of a merchant ship. Short, broad-shouldered, but not obese. Nautical garb. Beret with a light blue pompon. White Vandyke beard. White mustache.*
He	*Edgar Valpor, his son. About 30 years old. Clean-shaven. Good-looking.*
Small Son	*Tadzio, a boy 10 years old, with long blond hair.*
Lady	*Duchess Alice of Nevermore, a tall blonde, rather majestic and very beautiful, about 25 years old.*
Water Hen	*Elizabeth Gutzie-Virgeling, a person of unknown origin, about 26 years old. Flaxenhaired. Light eyes. Average height. Very pretty, but not at all seductive. Nose turned up just a little bit. Lips very wide, thick, and liver red.*
Scoundrel	*Richard de Korbowa-Korbowski, recte* Tom Hoozy, good-looking, dark-haired, very scoundrelly, about 20 years old. Looks like Edgar Valpor.*
Three Old Men: a. Ephemer Typowicz	*A businessman, clean-shaven, short gray hair, grown corpulent with power.*
b. Isaak Specter	*Tall, thin, grizzled Semite, with a black mustache and a Vandyke beard. Refined gestures, an Assyrian type.*
c. Alfred Evader	*Nervous, red-haired Semite, with gold pince-nez. Skinny and tall. A mustache, no trace of a beard, a typical Hittite.*
Footman	*Jan Parblichenko, an ordinary flunkey. Reddish-brown hair, pimply. Completely clean-shaven.*

* Witkiewicz uses the Latin *recte* and *false* throughout the play to indicate Hoozy's true and assumed names. [Translators' note]

Four More Footmen	*With long hair, two dark, two albino. All of them (including Jan) dressed in blue frock coats, shirts with ruffled fronts, and white stockings. They wear a great many military medals on their frock coats. Middle-aged. Jan is distinguished from the others by red aiguillettes.*
Three Detectives	*Head detective, Adolf Orsin, blond hair and a big mustache. One of the other two has a mustache and wears glasses. The other has a long black beard. They appear artificial and banal.*
Nanny	*Afrosia Yupupova, an old woman with a heart of gold. A fat blonde 40 years old.*
The Lamplighter	*A bearded individual in a workman's blue coat.*

Supplementary instructions from the central authority: speak without affectation and not from the guts, even at the worst moments.

ACT I

An open field, sparsely overgrown with juniper bushes. Some of the juniper bushes are shaped like cypress (two to the left and three to the right). Here and there bunches of yellow flowers (something in the poppy line). The horizon meets the edge of the sea. In the center of the stage a mound a little over three feet high. A crimson-colored pole (five feet high) rises from the mound. Hanging from the pole there is a very large octagonal lantern with green glass (the lantern may be silver and ornate). The Water Hen, wearing a chemise, stands under the pole. Her arms are bare. She has rather short hair, tied with a blue ribbon, forming a large topknot; the rest of her hair falls loosely around her head. A sheer black crinoline petticoat shows beneath her short skirt, and her legs are bare. "He" stands to the left, dressed in the style of the three bound men in the illustrated edition of Robinson Crusoe. *Three-cornered hat, boots with very wide tops turned down (eighteenth-century style). He is holding a double-barreled shotgun of the worst make. At this very moment he is loading it, with his back and side almost turned to the audience. To the left, a red sunset. The sky is covered with fantastic clouds.*

WATER HEN (*gently reproachful*) Couldn't you be a little quicker about it?

EDGAR (*finishing loading*) All right—I'm ready, I'm ready. (*Shoulders the gun and aims at her—a pause*) I can't. Damn it. (*He lowers the gun.*)

WATER HEN (*as before*) You're wearing us both out quite unnecessarily. We've already decided everything. I thought that after so much anguish we'd finally understood each other. And now you're hesitating again. Be a man. Hurry up and aim!

EDGAR (*raising his shotgun*) There's one thing I hadn't thought of. But what does it matter? (*Shoulders the gun and aims; a pause*) I can't. No, I can't pull the trigger. (*Lowers the gun*) The difficulty is that I won't have anyone to talk to any more. Who will I talk to if you're gone, Lizzie?

WATER HEN (*sighing*) Oh! You'll spend more time in your own company then. It will be very good for you. Be brave. Only for a moment. Afterward you'll be able to figure it out.

EDGAR (*sits on the ground in Turkish fashion*) But I don't want to be by myself.

WATER HEN (*sits resignedly on the mound*) You liked solitude in the old days. Do you remember how you used to run away from me? What's happened to you now?

EDGAR (*angrily*) I've grown accustomed to you. It's awful. I feel that there's a special kind of elastic band between us. I haven't been alone for the past two years. Even when you were far away, the elastic stretched, but never broke.

WATER HEN Well, try something different for once. I have nothing new to offer you. Your chances will be better without me. I'm not talking about women, but about things in general.

EDGAR You're trying to work on my baser instincts. Just like a woman. (*He jumps up.*) You must have a suicide mania. You're afraid yourself, and you use me like a piece of machinery. As if I were an extension of this shotgun. It's humiliating.

WATER HEN What a ridiculous idea! Death means nothing to me. That's the absolute truth. But I really don't want to die. Yet life means nothing to me either. What tires me most is standing here under this pole. (*The sun is setting, dusk is falling, and then it slowly turns dark.*)

EDGAR (*clutching the gun in his hands*) I can't stand this. You know what—let's stop all this and get away from here. This is a hateful place. Nothing can ever happen here.

WATER HEN (*gently*) No, Edgar, you have to make up your mind. It has to be decided today. We've already made up our minds. And that's all there is to it. I can't live the way I used to any more. Something's snapped inside me, and it will never come back again.

EDGAR (*groaning with indecision*) Hm. I hate to think what'll happen to me during the night. Boredom and suffering—a vicious circle, endless and self-contained and closed in upon itself forever. And there'll be no one to tell it to. After all, that's my only joy in life.

WATER HEN (*reproachfully*) Even at a time like this you're being small. But, honestly, you used to mean much more to me than I ever thought you could. You were my child and my father—something indefinable, something without form and without contour, filling my world with its indeterminateness. (*Changing her tone*) You're not a child, but you're so little, so hopelessly little . . .

EDGAR (*angrily*) Yes, I know. I'm not an undersecretary of state, a factory manager, a revolutionary, or a general. I'm a man without a profession and without a future. I'm not even an artist. At least artists know how to die in style.

WATER HEN Life for life's sake! Do you remember the theory of your friend the Duke of Nevermore? The so-called "creative life." Ha, ha!

EDGAR The insignificance of that concept is the cause of all my misfortunes. I waged a futile battle against myself for ten years, and after all that, you wonder why I can't make up my mind about such a trivial matter as killing you. Ha! Ha! (*He knocks the shotgun against the ground.*)

WATER HEN How stupid he is! Greatness is always irrevocable.

EDGAR There are limits to my endurance. Let's not have any contrived scenes. Even in the most idiotic plays it's definitely against the rules.

WATER HEN All right, but even you'll agree it's a vicious circle. Everything irrevocable is great, and that explains the greatness of death, first love, the loss of virginity, and so forth. Whatever one can do several times is by its very nature trivial. (*A pale gleam of moonlight shows through the clouds.*) You want to be great, and yet you don't want to do anything that can't be undone.

EDGAR (*ironically*) What about courage, self-sacrifice, suffering for someone else's sake, acts of renunciation? Aren't these forms of greatness too? But they're really not; as soon as you deny yourself something, you become so smug about your own greatness that it makes you petty. Every work of art is great because it's unique. Let's sacrifice ourselves for each other right now, or else join the circus.

WATER HEN (*ironically*) Anything that lives is unique, too, and hence great. You are great, Edgar, and so am I. If you don't shoot me this very minute, I'll despise you as an utter wet noodle.

EDGAR All this bores me. I'll shoot you like a dog. I hate you. You're my guilty conscience. It's I who despise you.

WATER HEN Let's not quarrel. I don't want to say good-bye to you in the middle of a scene. Come, kiss me on the forehead for the last time, and then shoot. We've thought it all out. Well, come on. (*After putting down the gun, Edgar approaches her hesitantly and kisses her on the forehead.*) And now go back to your place, my dear. Don't hesitate any more.

EDGAR (*goes to his former place stage left and picks up his shotgun*) Well, all right. It's all settled. I accept the inevitable. (*Examining the gun*)

WATER HEN (*clapping her hands*) Oh, how splendid!

EDGAR Stand still. (*The Hen stands still—Edgar shoulders the gun, aims for a long time, and fires from both barrels at short intervals. A pause.*)

WATER HEN (*still standing, her voice completely unchanged*) One miss. The other straight through the heart.

EDGAR (*silently ejects the cartridges from the shotgun and then slowly lays the gun on the ground and lights a cigarette*) There's one thing I've forgotten—what am I going to tell my father? Perhaps . . . (*While he is speaking, Tadzio crawls out from behind the mound, dressed in a boy's navy blue suit with a lace collar; he hides in the Hen's petticoats.*)

WATER HEN (*standing*) Go to your papa, Tadzio.

EDGAR (*turns around, notices Tadzio, and speaks with reluctance*) Oh, more surprises!

TADZIO Papa, Papa, don't be angry.

EDGAR I'm not angry, my child, I only want a little rest after all this. Where did you come from?

TADZIO I don't know. I woke up when I heard the shots. And you're my papa.

EDGAR Who knows? Maybe I'm a father, too. You see, my young man, it's all the same to me. For all I know, I might even be your father, although I can't stand children.

TADZIO But you won't beat me, Papa?

EDGAR (*somewhat dementedly*) I don't know, I don't know. (*Controlling himself*) You see, something's happened here. I can't tell you now. This woman (*pointing to the Hen*) in some way or other . . . Why am I telling you this?

TADZIO (*picking up the shotgun*) Please tell me, what were you shooting at?

EDGAR (*menacingly*) Put that down right now. (*Tadzio puts down the gun; more gently*) I was shooting because . . . How can I tell you? Well, you see I was . . .

WATER HEN (*in a weak voice*) Don't say anything . . . in just a moment . . .

EDGAR Yes, my boy, it's not as simple as you think. Assume I'm your father, if you will. But whoever your father may be, who is he really? What kind of a man will he turn out to be? These are still unanswered questions.

TADZIO But you're a grown-up, Papa, you know everything.

EDGAR Not as much as you think. (*To the Hen*) Something fatal's happened. I have so much to tell you that a whole lifetime wouldn't be long enough; then suddenly this little brat appears, and our last moments are hopelessly spoiled.

WATER HEN (*in a dying voice*) I'm dying. Remember what I told you. You must be great in one way or another.

EDGAR (*advances a few steps toward her*) Great, great, but how? At fishing or blowing soap bubbles?

WATER HEN (*weakly*) Don't come near me. This is the end. (*She slowly crumples on the mound. The moon behind the fleeting clouds occasionally lights up the stage. Now it shines rather brightly.*)

TADZIO Papa, what's the matter with that lady?

EDGAR (*signaling him to be quiet; not turning away from the Hen*) Quiet, wait. (*He gazes in silence at the Hen, who is expiring half-*

crumpled on the mound with her hands pressed to her breast. She breathes heavily and gives a death rattle. A cloud completely covers the moon. It is dark.)

TADZIO Papa, I'm afraid. It's scary here.

WATER HEN (*scarcely able to speak*) Go to him . . . I don't want . . . (*She dies. At this point the setting changes so that the field becomes the courtyard of a barracks. Two walls are slid in from the sides; a dim light appears in the center windows and at the gate below. At the same time Edgar comes up to Tadzio and silently puts his arms around him.*)

EDGAR Well, I am alone now. I can take care of you.

TADZIO I'm afraid. What happened to the lady?

EDGAR (*letting go of Tadzio*) I'll tell you the truth. She's dead.

TADZIO Dead? I don't know what dead means.

EDGAR (*surprised*) You don't know! (*Somewhat impatiently*) It's exactly as though she went to sleep, but she'll never wake up.

TADZIO Never! (*In a different tone of voice*) Never. I said I'd never steal apples, but that was different. Never—I understand now, it's the same forever and ever.

EDGAR (*impatiently*) Well, yes, that's the infinite, the eternal.

TADZIO I know God is infinite. I never could understand that. Papa, I know so much now. I understand everything. Only it's too bad about the lady. I'd like to tell her so.

EDGAR (*partly to himself, grimly*) There's a great deal I'd like to tell her, too. Much more than you.

TADZIO Papa, tell me the whole truth. Why won't you tell me? It's very important.

EDGAR (*waking up, after having been lost in his thoughts*) You're right. I have to tell you. There's no one else I can tell it to. (*Emphatically*) I killed her.

TADZIO You killed her? So you were the one who shot her. How funny! Ha, ha . . . As though you were out hunting.

EDGAR Tadzio, Tadzio, don't laugh like that. It's dreadful.

TADZIO (*becoming serious*) It's not dreadful at all, if it really happened the way you say it did. I was shooting, too, but at crows with a bird gun. You look so big, Papa. But it all seems as if some insects had eaten one another. People are like insects, and Infinity surrounds them and summons them in a mysterious voice.

EDGAR Where did you get that? Did you read it somewhere?

TADZIO Perhaps I dreamed it. I have such strange dreams. Please go on talking, Papa. I'll explain everything to you.

EDGAR (*sitting on the ground*) You see, it was like this. I should have been somebody, but I never knew what, or rather who. I don't even know whether I actually exist, although the fact that I suffer terribly is certainly real. That woman (*pointing backward with the index finger of his left hand*) wanted to help me; she was the one who asked me to kill her. Eventually all of us will die. Desperately unhappy people find consolation in that thought. (*Enter from stage right the Lamplighter; he lights the lantern. Eight concentric beams of intense green light fill the stage. Tadzio sits down next to Edgar —they talk to each other without paying any attention to the Lamplighter, who is listening to them.*) Why, why? If a man doesn't live like everybody else, if he doesn't work toward a goal, like a horse with blinders over his eyes walking around in a treadmill, then let me tell you Tadzio, quite truthfully, that he's completely in the dark. The goal is in the goal itself, as my friend Edgar, Duke of Nevermore, used to say. But I never could fathom that deep truth.

TADZIO (*nodding seriously*) Oh, I understand. I'm not satisfied with just anything, either, but right now I don't want anything at all, nothing at all—do you understand?

EDGAR (*putting his arms around him*) Oh, yes, I understand. You're starting pretty early, my young friend. What'll you be like when you're my age? (*The Lamplighter, who listened for a while, silently leaves through stage right.*)

TADZIO I'll be a robber.

EDGAR (*moving away from him in disgust*) Shut up. Don't talk that way. Sometimes I'd like to do something terrible, too.

TADZIO Ha, ha. How funny you are, Papa! There's really nothing terrible at all. Only there are certain times when it's best not to be afraid. And frightful things, really frightful things I paint in watercolors only—do you know what I mean? I have pastel colors like that, so I'm only really afraid when I'm asleep.

EDGAR (*jumping up*) Nothing happens, nothing. I thought that something would happen, but there's no change—the same silence everywhere, and the earth silently revolves on its axis. The world is a desert without meaning. (*He looks around him and notices the barracks.*) Look, Tadzio, I have the impression we're in prison. Yellow walls. (*Lights blink in the center windows of the barracks. Tadzio stands up and looks around him.*)

TADZIO I know this house. Soldiers are stationed here. The seashore is over there. (*He points to the gate of the barracks.*)

EDGAR (*disillusioned*) Oh, yes, I thought it was a prison. I feel like a dog on a chain who's been set free, but doesn't know how to run. For the rest of my life I'll walk around the kennel, and I won't have the courage to run away. Because—who knows?—I'll probably feel that perhaps it isn't true, I'm still on the chain. (*To Tadzio*) But tell me, once and for all, what were you doing here in the first place?

TADZIO (*after a moment's reflection*) I don't know, and I don't even want to remember. I was very ill in a kind of institution for boys. I didn't have a mother. And then I woke up as you were shooting, but I know this house, perhaps from my dreams.

EDGAR (*waves his hand contemptuously*) That's hardly very important. Tomorrow I'll begin your upbringing. (*At this moment Edgar's Father, wearing nautical garb, enters from stage right; he stops and listens to Edgar and Tadzio without being noticed by them.*)

TADZIO You'll never be able to bring me up, Papa. You couldn't.

EDGAR Why?

TADZIO You've had no upbringing yourself. I know that much about you at least.

FATHER (*coming up to them*) You talk very well, Sonny boy. (*To Edgar*) Where did you unearth such a precocious little imp?

EDGAR (*getting up*) I don't know. He crept out from behind that mound. (*The Father turns around and notices the Water Hen's dead body.*)

FATHER What's this? (*With a wave of his hand*) After all, it hardly matters. I don't meddle in your personal affairs. The Water Hen is dead. Since there'll be no supper at home, I trust you'll approve of our having something to eat here. I'll give orders to have the body carried out. I can't stand corpses flopping about where they have no business to be. (*He blows his whistle, which he wears on a yellow string. Edgar and Tadzio remain standing silently.*)

TADZIO This is funny. I can see myself painting it in pastels and even then . . . (*Four footmen rush in and fall in in a row.*)

FATHER (*pointing to the Hen's corpse*) Carry the lady out. There ought to be a cold cellar somewhere in this barracks. (*He uses his finger to point to one of the footmen.*) Tell the orderly that I'll send for the corpse tomorrow. Don't ask any questions, and don't go blabbing about it. And then bring a table here and serve supper.

FOOTMEN Yes, we understand. At your service. (*They immediately pounce on the Hen's corpse and carry her out stage left.*)

FATHER (*to Tadzio*) Well, young man, how do you like all this? Huh?

TADZIO It's really hilarious. Still there's something missing. I don't know what.

EDGAR Father, won't you leave him in peace? I've adopted him. I'll take care of the formalities tomorrow. I'm beginning another life. Not a new life, but another one—do you understand, Father?

FATHER You can even start at the end and go backward. You can't escape. Gauguin didn't begin to paint until he was twenty-seven, Bernard Shaw didn't begin to write plays until after he was thirty. But what's the point of giving examples? I tell you you'll be an artist, just as sure as I'm Albert Valpor, former skipper of the *Orenteso,* a vessel of ten thousand tons. Our story today is only the beginning—but a promising one. Own up to it, Ed, you killed the Water Hen.

EDGAR Yes, I did. But she asked me to.

FATHER Naturally. She preferred death to living with you. And yet she couldn't live without you. Poor silly Hen. I'm sorry about it. But what'll you do now? Who'll listen to your long, pedantic lectures justifying your downfall? Eh? Perhaps this young ward of yours. Huh?

TADZIO How wise you are, Captain! Papa has gone over everything with me. (*The Footmen bring in a table from stage left, place it before the mound, and set it for five people. A simple table, simple wicker chairs.*)

FATHER Didn't I tell you so? You've had a rendez-vous with destiny, my adopted grandson. Edgar Valpor, the great artist of the future, has taken you into his confidence. Never forget that.

EDGAR Must you joke, Father? This is hardly an appropriate time. (*He notices the table.*) Why so many place settings?

FATHER I'm expecting guests. I want to provide you with enemies disguised as friends and, vice versa, friends disguised as the bitterest enemies. You don't know how to live simply and normally, so you'll have to live your life in reverse and walk backward along wayward paths. My patience is at an end. I've had enough.

EDGAR And so Father you . . . (*Tadzio plays with the double-barreled shotgun.*)

FATHER Yes, yes, I knew what would happen. I foresaw a great deal. Not everything, of course. I didn't know you'd shoot her. Now I don't want to spoil you. Still I must admit that I'm somewhat impressed. Somewhat, I repeat, despite the fact that you've behaved like a thoroughly cheap stinker.

EDGAR You're not a man, you're a devil. So you knew all along, Father?

FATHER There's nothing remarkable about that. Don't you remember when the three of us lived in the little house on the other side of the bay at Stockfish Beach? Remember her mania for feeding lemons to my ginger cat? I was able to observe the two of you very closely then. You both thought I was only searching for buried treasure. Remember, when she gave you that purple flower and said, "A great man does not ask how to become great, he is great." I even wrote it down.

EDGAR Don't say anything more, Father. Poor Elizabeth, poor Water Hen. (*He covers his face with his hands.*)

TADZIO (*comes up to him with the shotgun in his hand*) Don't cry, Papa. These are only little pictures God paints with his magic pastels.

EDGAR (*opens his eyes and notices the gun*) Take it away! I cannot bear to look at that thing. (*He grabs the gun out of Tadzio's hands and throws it to the right. All this time the Footmen pay no attention and set the table.*)

FATHER Easy. Easy. Ham—bleeding heart—sentimental ass. (*Edgar stands still staring at the ground.*) Remember you're leading another life. Another life—as you've so aptly put it. Go live on Mars or on the star Antares if you can't get along here. My guests are about to arrive, do you understand? Don't you dare let me down with that hang-dog look! Don't you forget it! (*Nonsensical sounds from an accordion are heard from the right.*) They're coming. (*To Edgar*) Chin up. Not a whimper!

TADZIO Captain, you're wonderful! Like an evil sorcerer.

FATHER (*moved*) Call me grandfather. At last there's someone who appreciates my style. (*He strokes Tadzio's head. The accordion playing gets closer.*)

EDGAR (*explaining*) I appreciate your style, too. I just don't want you to jump to conclusions about . . .

FATHER Then don't let me jump over you as if I were a horse and you were a hurdle. Silence. The guests are coming.

(*Duchess Alice enters from stage right. She is dressed in a ball gown the color of the sea. She wears a scarf, but no hat. She is followed by Tom Hoozy [false Korbowa-Korbowski Richard], dressed in a frock coat without a hat; he enters playing the accordion. Three old men come in after them.*)

LADY How do you do, Captain? (*Father kisses her hand, playing the young man. Hoozy has stopped playing the accordion and observes the situation.*)

FATHER My dear lady—so delighted to see you. The situation here is rather snarled, but we can unsnarl it. It was hardly necessary for the Duchess to bring these gentlemen. (*Points to the old men*) However, we'll have to do the best we can.

LADY But these gentlemen are quite charming. Let me introduce them to you.

FATHER Oh, we already know one another. (*He greets the old men in a perfunctory manner*.) And now, if your Grace will allow me, I'll present to you my son, who was a great friend of your late husband. Ed, greet Her Grace. My son—Duchess Alice of Nevermore.

EDGAR Good heavens, is Edgar dead?

FATHER We'll talk about it later—behave yourself.

EDGAR (*kisses the Duchess' hand*) Please tell me what happened to Edgar.

LADY A tiger devoured him in Janjapara Jungle. He was always putting his courage to the test until finally the Supreme Being lost his patience. He died two days after the accident, and I assure you he died beautifully. His belly was torn to pieces, and he suffered terribly. But up to the last moment he was reading Russell and Whitehead's *Principia Mathematica*. You know—all those symbols.

EDGAR Yes, I know. What strength! Poor Edgar. (*To his father*) Why didn't you tell me about it before, Father? I'm buffeted by so many blows all at once. My God, did Elizabeth know about it?

LADY Has anything else happened? Tell me. I've heard so much about you from Edgar. He considered you the most interesting character on the face of our small globe.

EDGAR Yes—something strange has happened. I'm on the threshold of another life. Beyond the grave almost . . .

FATHER That's enough. As a matter of fact, today he shot the Water Hen like a dog. At her own request. Wouldn't you agree, Duchess, that's a lousy thing to do?

LADY Oh, that Elizabeth Virgeling! I've heard so much about you two from Edgar! My poor husband often received letters from her. She wrote such strange things. Afterward he was never quite himself.

FATHER I'd still like to know whether or not you think it's a lousy thing to do.

LADY But Mr. Albert—women love to sacrifice themselves: what good luck to have the chance to die for someone else. Isn't that so, Mr. . . . Edgar? It's strange to say that name again.

EDGAR Well, yes . . . I suppose so . . . I don't know. I killed her half an hour ago.

LADY What a pity. I so much wanted to meet her.

EDGAR Edgar was in love with her and worshiped her from a distance. He wrote me that she was the only woman he could really . . .

LADY (*dissatisfied, she interrupts him*) Edgar loved only me, my dear sir. (*Tadzio stands to the left and looks at everyone delightedly*.)

EDGAR But, my dear lady, I'll show you Edgar's letters.

LADY That doesn't mean anything at all. He was lying. Let's go for a stroll, and I'll explain everything to you. (*All this time the Footmen have been standing stiffly between the mound and the table. The Lady and Edgar pass to the left. The Father stands looking now at the old men and Hoozy, now at them. As she passes by)* Who's this charming little boy?

EDGAR That's my adopted son. I adopted him exactly twenty minutes ago.

LADY *(smiling)* Half an hour ago you killed her. Twenty minutes ago you adopt some boy or other. It seems to me you've really been through enough for one day. Edgar told me you were strong as Hercules. What's your name, little boy?

TADZIO My name is Tadeusz Gutzie-Virgeling. *(To the Duchess)* You're a very beautiful woman. Like the fortuneteller in the picture I drew.

EDGAR What? That too? I'll go out of my mind.

FATHER *(bursts out laughing)* Ha, ha, ha. That's a good one. *(He beats his hands rapidly up and down on his knees.)*

EDGAR Did you know about that too, father? You knew Elizabeth had a son, and you didn't tell me anything about it?

FATHER *(laughing)* As sure as I am the skipper of the *Oronteso*, I knew nothing about it. It's a surprise to me. Come here, Tadzio, let me give you a hug. *(Tadzio goes to him.)*

EDGAR What was it you wanted to tell me?

LADY I want to prove to you that it's all a mistake. *(They pass to the left and whisper. Hoozy plays the accordion impatiently.)*

EVADER Mr. Specter, this is an extraordinary affair. I think we'd better go have supper at the Astoria. Or else we'll have to face the consequences.

SPECTER Take my word for it, Mr. Evader. Nothing bad's going to happen.

FATHER *(lets go of Tadzio)* But, gentlemen, please stay to supper, they'll set the table for you right away. *(To a Footman)* Get a move on! Three more place settings and more wine; hurry up! *(The Footmen dash to the left.)* Tonight we'll drink till we all fall overboard. Isn't that right, Mr. Korbowski? You were in the navy.

KORBOWSKI *(produces a wild sob from the accordion)* All right, Mr. Valpor. But I don't like that flirtation between Alice and your only son. *(Points to the left)* She's no morsel for degenerates, my Alice isn't! Alice is mine! *(He throws down his accordion, which gives a wail. The others turn around.)*

EVADER Mr. Specter, let's go.

SPECTER I quite agree. I smell trouble.

TYPOWICZ Wait! We're invited to supper. It's an amusing situation.

EDGAR (*to the Lady*) Who's that swine? Oh, excuse me—he came with you, but after all . . .

LADY (*passing to the right*) He's my only consolation in life. Mr. Korbowski—Mr. Edgar Valpor. (*The men greet each other; the Footmen set three new places at the table.*) He's utterly primitive. If it weren't for him, I wouldn't have survived Edgar's death. We met in India. Now we go everywhere together and see the most revolting things in the world. You have no idea how beautifully he conducts himself in every situation.

KORBOWSKI Alice, darling, please don't joke. You're twisting the lion's tail. I want to be treated with respect whether we're in company or alone.

EDGAR Why is he so familiar with you? What's going on?

KORBOWSKI I'm this lady's lover. Understand? I was invited here by your father, and no uncouth only son is going to get in my way. (*The Duchess looks at both of them through her lorgnette.*)

EDGAR Don't go too far . . . or I won't be responsible for my actions. I've had enough for today. Please. (*The Footmen have set the table and stand in a row behind it.*)

KORBOWSKI I'm not going to let Alice carry on with the first ameba who happens to come along. I'm her lover, and I draw a yearly salary of forty thousand francs—with the approval of the late Duke Edgar.

EDGAR So you're just a kept man, an ordinary Alphonse . . .

KORBOWSKI (*coldly, with passion*) I'm not Alphonse, I'm Richard, and a quite extraordinary one at that. Take a good look at that. (*He shoves his fist under Edgar's nose.*)

EDGAR What? Shoving your filthy paw in my face! (*He strikes Korbowski between the eyes with his fist. A short fight.*)

KORBOWSKI You only son . . .

EDGAR Take that and that! I'll show you! (*He throws Hoozy out stage right and runs out after him.*)

LADY (*to Father*) Why, your son is an athlete! He overpowered Korbowski! And besides he's so good-looking. The photograph doesn't do him justice. It lacks expression. And what intelligence! I've read his letters to Edgar.

FATHER (*bowing*) It's only nervous energy. I never could persuade him to do his morning exercises. Nerves. Nervous energy. The way madmen in an asylum break their cell bars. Yes, nerves. We're descended from old nobility.

LADY Why, with nerves like that, who needs an athlete's muscles? What a magnificent specimen of masculinity!

FATHER I was sure your Grace would be pleased.

LADY Call me daughter, Mr. Valpor. It's all settled. (*The Father bows. Edgar comes back.*)

EDGAR (*the ruffles of his shirt are crumpled—without his hat*) Do you know what he was shouting as he ran away? That you (*pointing to the Duchess*) couldn't live without him and his evil ways, his rotten tricks, to be more precise, as he himself put it. He claims that you're an utterly depraved woman. So did Edgar.

LADY (*coquettishly*) Find out for yourself. Starting tomorrow, I'm going to be your wife. Your father's already given his consent.

EDGAR So soon? I don't really know who I am yet. Perhaps in a day or two.

FATHER Idiot, when you can get something for nothing, take it, and don't ask questions. Such a high-class woman, and yet he hesitates.

LADY (*to Father*) It's only bashfulness. (*To Edgar*) I'm sure you'll be happy with me. We've already become acquainted through all those letters and also because of what Edgar himself told me. He actually brought us together a long time ago, although he loved only me. Please believe me.

EDGAR But I do believe you, I have to. (*Takes her by the hand*) Is it really true? Can I start another life?

LADY Yes, with me. With me everything is possible.

EDGAR But that Korbowski. I'm afraid of what he's got in mind . . .

LADY Don't be afraid. With you I'm not afraid of anything. (*She takes his head in her hands and kisses him.*)

TADZIO Grandfather, will I really get such a beautiful mother?

FATHER Yes, my boy. You've won first prize. She's a genuine English Duchess. (*To everybody*) And now, gentlemen, we can sit down to supper. Please. (*He points to the table. Tadzio comes up to the Lady, who hugs him.*)

LADY My child, from now on you may call me mama.

EDGAR (*deep in thought, near the front of the stage, partly to himself*) My friend's wife—my mistress's son. At last I've created a family for myself! But won't it be too much for me? (*To his Father*) Listen to me, Father. Should I humor myself this way? Shouldn't I undergo some kind of penance first?

FATHER Sit down at the table and don't bother me.

EDGAR (*to everybody, as though justifying himself*) It's people and circumstances that have always made me what I am. I'm a manikin, a marionette. Before I can create anything, everything happens all by itself exactly the way it always has, and not because of anything I've done. What is this? Some sort of a curse?

LADY You can tell me all about it later. Now let's go eat. I'm desperately hungry. (*They sit down.*)

ACT II

A salon in Nevermore palace. To the left by the wall, a round table.
Armchairs. There are no windows. Door to the left and to the right.
Pictures on the walls. Everything in strawberry hues which gradually
become suffused with a warm blue. In the center a wide niche and
three steps which end in four thin columns made of rosy-orange
marble. Behind the columns a dark cherry curtain. To the left, in the
armchair, three-fourths turned toward the auditorium, the Lady sits
doing embroidery. Her small son is playing on the carpet, constructing
some fairly large mechanical device. His hair is cut short and looks
velvety, and he is wearing a dark carmine suit. The Lady is wearing a
silver-gray dress. Dusk is slowly falling. A moment of silence.

TADZIO (*without stopping his tinkering*) Mama, I forgot why He's my
   papa.
LADY It doesn't make any difference if you have. No one knows why
   things are the way they are and not some other way. You can ask
   such questions endlessly and never find any answers.
TADZIO I know—Infinity. I'll never forget how I first came to understand what it means. Ever since then everything's really been all
   right. I think everything's infinite and has to be the way it is. But
   there's just one thing: why exactly is He my papa and not someone
   else?
LADY Perhaps you'd prefer to have Mr. Korbowski as your papa, my
   little philosopher?
TADZIO Don't talk to me like that, Mama. I'll tell you something else: as
   soon as you appeared, I forgot everything that had happened before.
   It's like one of those dreams you can never recall. I remember only
   my name. Nothing else.
LADY That's a great deal. Apparently you had to forget everything
   else.
TADZIO I want to find out how I came to be: where I came from and
   where everything's going. Things keep on going all by themselves
   and seem to be heading somewhere. What's it all about? Where's it
   all rushing so fast?
LADY (*slightly disconcerted*) Ask your father. Even I don't know that.
TADZIO Mother, you're keeping something from me. But I know more
   than I'm letting on. Your eyes are double, like those little boxes with
   a secret drawer.
LADY Now it's my turn to say: don't talk to me like that. I'm very fond
   of you, and I don't want to have to hurt you.
TADZIO Haven't I been good? Nothing seems right. Everything's hap-

pening as if I were dreaming. (*With sudden animation*) You know, I've never been afraid of anything except in my dreams. And now that everything seems like a dream, I'm really afraid that at any moment something dreadful will happen and I'll be much more terrified than I ever was in any dream. I feel so frightened sometimes. I'm afraid of fear. (*Jan Parblichenko enters and lights the electric candelabra hanging from the ceiling.*)

LADY Jan, has the Master returned?

JAN Not yet, Your Grace.

LADY Don't forget the special liqueurs. There'll be guests for dinner.

JAN Yes, Your Grace.

TADZIO (*standing up*) So there'll be more of those repulsive characters who torment papa. (*Jan leaves stage left.*)

LADY (*somewhat venomously*) And Mr. Korbowski will be here.

TADZIO He's a man out of a bad dream. But I like him. I like to look at him. He's like a snake who eats small birds.

LADY (*ironically*) And you're a small bird, aren't you?

TADZIO Mama, why do you talk to me the way you would to a grown-up? I asked you not to talk that way.

LADY I never had any children, and I don't know how to talk to them. If you want to, go to Afrosia.

TADZIO She doesn't have double eyes. Still she bores me. I don't like good people, but bad people make me suffer.

LADY (*smiling*) Am I bad?

TADZIO I don't know. But you make me suffer, Mama, and I like to be with you because you make me suffer.

LADY (*with a smile*) What perversity!

TADZIO That's a word for a grown-up. I know. Why can't I wake up? Everything seems wrong somehow. (*Jan enters from the right.*)

JAN Mr. Korbowski, Your Grace.

LADY Ask him to come in. (*Exit Jan. Tadzio becomes silent, his gaze fixed on the door to the right. Korbowski enters wearing a frock coat.*)

KORBOWSKI Good evening. Am I late?

LADY No, dinner is late. Edgar hasn't come back yet.

KORBOWSKI (*kisses her hand and sits down next to her facing forward*) Alice, how can you call that soggy wet noodle by the same name as your husband, the late Duke? I may not be very refined, but it gives me a kind of psychological ache. (*Tadzio makes a gesture as though he wanted to throw himself on Korbowski, but he restrains himself.*)

LADY (*with a smile*) Well—as long as it's not physical, you can stand it.

KORBOWSKI Don't laugh. I wear my soul in a sling like a broken arm, like fruit stolen out of my own garden which my enemy has leased. I feel a morganatic attraction for you, strong as an American tornado. I am consumed with passion for a misalliance, transformed by a clever writer into a self-libel, with which I flog my own impotent destiny.

LADY But there's no sense at all to anything you're saying.

KORBOWSKI I know, that's why I say it. I read night and day, and my head is spinning. (*He stretches his legs out, leaning his head back behind the armchair.*)

LADY Sit up properly.

KORBOWSKI I don't have the strength. I'm like a shirt that's been embraced by a wringer. I'm afraid of time whirling past me like the wind on the pampas around the rushing antelope. I'm exhausted.

TADZIO (*seriously*) You put that very nicely. When I wake up from this dream, I'll paint it.

KORBOWSKI Listen, young aesthete, suppose you go to sleep? Really and truly, to bed, huh?

TADZIO (*leaning against the Lady's armchair*) I won't go. You're just a handsome tramp, and this is my home.

KORBOWSKI You're as much of a tramp as I am. Go to sleep, that's my advice.

LADY Mr. Korbowski is right. Both of you have an equal right to be here with me.

TADZIO That's not true. If I knew why He's my papa, I'd answer you differently. It's a mystery.

KORBOWSKI There's no mystery at all. Your so-called father is a common murderer. He may be hanged at any moment. He lives by the grace of the Duchess, like a dog on a chain. Understand?

TADZIO That's not true. If he wanted to, papa could be great, but he doesn't want to. I heard that somewhere.

KORBOWSKI (*gets up and pushes Tadzio away brutally*) You little moron, I'll give you greatness! Clear out! (*Tadzio falls down on the carpet, crawls up to the machine, and starts to operate it again, stooping over—not saying anything. Korbowski stands bending over the Lady.*) Alice! I can't take it any longer. You don't belong here. Throw that Valpor out once and for a tired wet noodle. I can't go on living like this. I can feel something new and strange, something colossally rotten growing inside me, and it'll be nasty for anyone who gets in my way. Understand? Everything I read (and I don't do anything else) I eagerly pervert into evil—odious, hairy, cruel, red-hot evil. Don't push me over the brink. Will you leave all this and come with me now? I don't want to go back to being what I was without you. I know I'm nothing. What are you paying me for? Why do I go on living? (*He clutches his head in his hands.*)

TADZIO (*turns around and looks at him ecstatically*) Blow up, Mr. Korbowski, go ahead and blow up. (*The Lady bursts out laughing.*)

KORBOWSKI (*shaking his fist at him*) Shut up! (*To the Lady*) Alice, I'm nothing at all—that's just it! That's why I used to be the happiest man in the world. Now that I have everything I've always dreamed about, it all seems worthless without you. I might as well put a bullet through my head. I'll go stark raving mad!

LADY (*coldly*) Have you been unfaithful to me?

KORBOWSKI No, no, no! Don't question me about it so casually. I can't stand it.

LADY He's suffering, too.

KORBOWSKI What's that to me? Let him go on suffering in peace and quiet. You've turned this house into a colossal torturtorium. I don't want any part of it.

LADY (*with a smile*) Then go away!

KORBOWSKI (*bending over her*) I can't. Will you leave all this and come with me now! (*Jan enters.*)

JAN Messieurs Specter, Evader, and Typowicz, Your Grace.

LADY Show them in. (*Exit Jan. Enter the three old men wearing frock coats.*)

KORBOWSKI (*bending over her embroidery, aloud*) What lovely needlework! The blues and yellows complement each other so exquisitely. (*Softly, through his teeth*) Will you leave all this and come with me now!

LADY (*gets up, passes by him, and goes to greet the old men*) Gentlemen, you'll forgive us, Edgar is late. (*The old men kiss the Lady's hand.*)

TYPOWICZ Oh, that's all right. But how are we doing with our new venture, The Theosophical Jam Company?

LADY We're putting up all our capital. We'll secure the balance with real estate as collateral. Even the name is marvelous. Edgar has gone to the Union Bank. He should be back any minute.

KORBOWSKI Alice!

LADY (*turning away, in a cold voice*) Mr. Korbowski, must I ask you to leave our house? (*Korbowski rolls up into a ball and falls into an armchair, covering his face with his hands.*)

TYPOWICZ Dear Lady, this is a great day for the corporation.

EVADER You're the only member of the aristocracy who . . .

SPECTER (*interrupts him*) Yes—you alone had the courage. Your example ought to . . .

LADY I can't talk about all this before dinner. Gentlemen, please sit down. (*Goes to the left; the old men follow her; they sit down without greeting Korbowski*) I'm in favor of a total Semitico-Aryan coalition. The Semites are the race of the future.

EVADER Yes. The spiritual rebirth of the Jews is the key to the future happiness of mankind.

SPECTER We'll show what we can do as a race. Up until now we've produced only individual geniuses.

(*The curtain in the back is drawn, and Edgar quickly runs down the stairs, dressed in a black frock coat. Tadzio flings himself toward him.*)

TADZIO Papa, I can't stand it any more! I don't know when she's telling the truth. (*He points to the Lady.*)

EDGAR (*shoving him away*) Go away. (*To everybody*) Dinner is served.

TADZIO Papa, I'm so all alone. (*Edgar talks with the old men, paying no attention to Tadzio. Korbowski sits like a mummy.*)

LADY (*rings; Afrosia, dressed entirely in green, runs in from the left side of the stage; a green scarf on her head*) Afrosia Ivanovna, take this child away. See that he drinks his herb tea and put him to bed!

(*Afrosia takes Tadzio by the hand, and they go off to the left. From the right-hand side of the stage the Water Hen enters, dressed as in Act I, but wearing silk stockings, patent leather pumps, and a cape thrown over her shoulders.*)

LADY And who is this?

EDGAR (*turning around*) It's she! You're alive?

WATER HEN That should hardly be any concern of yours.

TADZIO (*stopping at the door to the left—shouts*) Mama! (*He runs to the Hen.*)

EDGAR (*to the Hen*) Is he your son? You lied about everything.

WATER HEN (*astounded*) I have never lied. I don't know this boy at all. (*She pushes Tadzio away, and he clings to her.*)

TADZIO Mama! You don't know me?

WATER HEN Calm down, child. I never was your mother.

TADZIO So I have no one at all! (*He cries.*) And I can't wake up.

EDGAR Afrosia Ivanovna, take Tadzio out of here this very minute, see that he goes to bed immediately. (*Afrosia takes Tadzio away to the left; as he goes, he is convulsed with tears.*)

LADY (*nudging Edgar*) Tell me, who is that woman?

EDGAR It's the Water Hen—Elizabeth Virgeling.

LADY But what does this mean? You killed her.

EDGAR Apparently not, since she just walked in and is standing right there. That would appear to be fairly conclusive evidence.

KORBOWSKI (*getting up*) So she's really alive! I'm ruined. There goes my last chance of getting rid of that bad dream! (*To Edgar*) Rest assured, Mr. Valpor, the attempted blackmail didn't work.

EDGAR You and your blackmail mean nothing to me. I tolerate your presence here in this house of my own free will. I'm devoting my entire life now to penance. (*To the Hen*) Penance for what I've failed to accomplish. I failed, and I've got to suffer for it and do penance. You should be delighted—it's all your fault. Can you imagine anything worse?

WATER HEN You're still not suffering enough. Not nearly enough. And that's why everything seems so awful to you. (*Father enters from the right-hand side of the stage, in a frock coat, his beard shaved.*)

EDGAR Oh, Father, please look after the guests. I want to talk privately with this woman. It's the Water Hen—she's alive! Judging by your complete lack of surprise, I suppose you knew exactly what was going to happen.

FATHER (*cheerfully*) Well, of course.

EDGAR You monster!

FATHER Your late mother spoiled you. I've got to make up for it, so I'm bringing you up in my own way. And now, ladies and gentlemen, will you please come to the dining room. (*To the Lady*) Alice—has Mr. de Korbowa-Korbowski been invited, too?

LADY Of course. (*To the Hen*) After you've talked with my husband, please join us at the table. And after dinner you and I will have a little chat.

WATER HEN And who are you, may I ask?

LADY I am Edgar Valpor's wife and Edgar Nevermore's widow. Apparently you're the one woman my husband was in love with, from a distance of a thousand miles. Ha, ha! (*To the guests*) Please come, gentlemen. (*Korbowski offers her his arm. She motions him away and offers her arm to Typowicz. They go up the stairs. Jan draws the curtain. The two old men follow them, the Father comes next, and in the rear Korbowski drags along, completely shattered. All this while Edgar and the Hen stand still, looking at each other. All the others disappear behind the curtain, which is then drawn shut.*)

WATER HEN Do you love her?

EDGAR Don't even say that word in my presence. I hate the very sound of it.

WATER HEN Once and for all, answer my question.

EDGAR No, no, that's an entirely different matter. I'm just a marionette. I'm outside of whatever happens to me. And I watch myself like a Chinese shadow moving on a screen. I can only observe the movements, but have no control over them.

WATER HEN So nothing has happened as a result of my death?

EDGAR What's happened is that I suffer a thousand times more than I ever did. I've started another life—not a new one. I gave that up a long time ago. ANOTHER LIFE! I'm creating a new skeleton inside of what already exists. Or rather they are—my father and the Duchess.

WATER HEN And the utter void? I mean as far as feelings are concerned.

EDGAR It goes on and on.

WATER HEN What does your father expect of you? The same as always?

EDGAR Yes, he says I'll certainly become an artist.

WATER HEN But you have no talent—not for anything whatever.

EDGAR That's precisely the point. I don't have any and never will. It's as impossible as changing one's complexion. Black hair can be bleached, but can a black character?

WATER HEN Will you be angry if I ask you something: How's the greatness problem coming?

EDGAR Greatness? Monstrosity perhaps? I've already told you: I'm a buffoon, a plaything of unknown forces. I'm great—like a marionette. Ha, ha!

WATER HEN Don't laugh. What about real life?

EDGAR I manage my wife's estate; I've invested all of it in the Theosophical Jam Company. Those three men are making all the arrangements. I'm only a manikin. (*A pause*)

WATER HEN Don't get angry if I tell you something. You're not suffering enough.

EDGAR You dare say that to me? Don't you understand how absolutely ghastly my life is?

WATER HEN I understand, but it's really nothing, nothing at all. The only way to get anything out of you is to torture you. I know what I'm talking about.

EDGAR Haven't I suffered enough already? My wife keeps that Korbowski in constant tow. The slimy maggot! I hate him, I loathe him, I despise him, and yet I have to put up with him all the time. Now he'll be on the board of the new company. I don't know whether he's her lover or not; I don't ask, I don't want to find out. Isn't that enough for you? All my evenings are pinnacles of utter degradation.

WATER HEN But you don't love her.

EDGAR You're a woman, my dear. You'll never understand. For you women it's only: he loves me, he loves me not, he loves me, he loves me not. You never understand suffering any more complicated than the wrong answer to that question.

WATER HEN Go on. What else makes you suffer?

EDGAR You know how I hate reality. From early morning on I'm up to my ears in business: board meetings at banks, the stock exchange, negotiations with wholesalers and big accounts. Now it's really starting. Imagine me, Edgar, a businessman! It's the height of agony.

WATER HEN It's not enough. A propos, what about Tadzio?

EDGAR Your deathbed bequest . . .

WATER HEN I swear I never saw that boy before.

EDGAR The facts are against you. But I don't want to go over that old story again. Besides, facts don't interest me. So you're not his mother?

WATER HEN But you know I can't be a mother!

EDGAR Miracles happen. Did you know they've built a huge barracks where I once tried to kill you without much success? But no matter.

WATER HEN Tell me, what's the relationship between you?

EDGAR Between Tadzio and me? Frankly, I'm insanely attached to him, but I have a deep suspicion that he'll grow up to be a scoundrel so monstrous that Korbowski will seem a saint by comparison. Along with my insane attachment to him, I feel an unbearable physical disgust. He doesn't love me at all and doesn't want to regard me as his father. He admires Korbowski—he's his artistic ideal. Now I've listed my principal sufferings. Isn't that enough?

WATER HEN That's nothing.

JAN (appears from behind the curtain): Her Grace requests that you come to the table.

EDGAR Right away. (Jan disappears.) That's nothing? What more do you want?

WATER HEN I don't know . . . Perhaps a prison sentence or maybe physical pain will cure you. There have been cases of conversion . . .

EDGAR To what? Theosophy?

WATER HEN No—to a belief in the positive values of life.

EDGAR Wait! Physical pain. That's a new idea! (He runs over to the table and rings. The Hen watches him curiously. Four Footmen run in from the left.) Listen to me: go to the Duchess' museum immediately and bring me the Spanish instrument of torture, you know, the one with the green and yellow stripes. Hurry. (The Footmen leave quickly stage left. Edgar paces up and down nervously. The Hen goes to the left, sits down in an armchair, and follows him with her eyes.)

EDGAR Well, now I'll show you . . .

WATER HEN Just don't lie to yourself.

EDGAR Quiet! Now I'm master of my own fate. I know what I'm doing, and I'll do it myself without anyone else's help. (Stamping his foot on the floor) Quiet! I tell you . . . (The Footmen come in carrying a box eight feet long, the sides of which are latticed with yellow and *green strips of board; at the corners there are yellow wheels which are connected to cranks; inside there is a small bench, and thick ropes hang from the cranks; the box looks very old.*) Set it down in the middle of the room! (*The Footmen put the box down and stand very stiffly by its four corners.*) And now listen to me: you'll torture me with this machine. No matter how much I cry out and beg for mercy, you're to stretch me till I stop screaming. Do you understand? Tie my hands and legs and then turn the cranks.

FOOTMEN Yes sir, all right, we understand.

EDGAR Well—hurry up! (*He takes off his frock coat and throws it on the ground; he is wearing a bluish shirt; then he quickly climbs into the box and lies down on the bench, his head to the left.*) Hurry! (*The Footmen tie the ropes with frantic speed and begin to turn the cranks, at first rapidly, then slowly, with effort. Edgar starts to groan horribly at regular intervals. The Hen laughs demonically in her armchair. When Edgar is not groaning, her laughter can clearly be heard.*)

EDGAR Stop—aaa! I can't stand it! Aaa! Aaa! Mercy! Enough! Aaa! (*He croaks the last "Aaa" horribly and is suddenly silent. The curtain is drawn, and the Lady can be seen looking in. The men crowd behind her. The Footmen stop and look into the box, without letting go of the cranks, which remain in the same position.*)

WATER HEN What are you gaping at? Keep on turning it. (*The company from the dining room comes slowly down into the drawing room, with the Lady leading the way. Jan follows them. The Hen stops laughing and sits quietly, staring madly straight ahead.*)

FOOTMAN I He's fainted.

FOOTMAN II He's had enough, poor fellow.

FATHER (*runs over to the box and looks into it*) Has he gone mad, or what? (*To the Footmen*) Get him out of there! (*The Footmen untie Edgar with frantic speed and pull him out, absolutely limp.*) Put him on the couch. (*To the Hen*) Elizabeth, was this hideous business your idea? (*At this moment, from the left side of the stage, Tadzio, in a nightshirt and stockings, runs in with a cry. Afrosia follows him. The Lady and her staff stay where they are, a little to the right. The Footmen carry Edgar to a small red couch, to the right, and stand erect to the right of it. Jan goes over to them. They whisper.*)

TADZIO Papa, papa! Don't cry like that ever again! (*He falls on his knees by the couch, on the far side to the rear of the stage; Edgar opens his eyes and his face brightens.*) Papa, I love you, I woke up from my dream. (*Edgar strokes his head.*) Papa, she's the one who's torturing you, that strange lady who didn't want to be my mother. I don't want her here. Take her away. (*He buries his head in Edgar's chest; Edgar hugs him.*)

KORBOWSKI (*speaks at the top of his voice in the midst of the silence*) This is barren metaphysical suffering in the fourth dimension.

FATHER Silence. (*To the Footmen*) Take that damned box out of here. Hurry up. (*The Footmen fling themselves at the box and carry it off to the left. Afrosia stands silently to the left. Edgar's black frock coat remains in the middle of the stage on the ground until the end of the act.*)

WATER HEN (*gets up and speaks to the Lady in a fiery voice*) Do you think that Edgar Nevermore loved you? He loved only me. I have his letters right here. I want you to know everything. I've always kept them with me, but now they're useless. (*She throws down a packet of letters at the Lady's feet. The packet becomes untied, and the letters scatter about. Korbowski picks them up eagerly.*)

LADY I know all that, and I've already proved to my second husband that your theory's wrong. You were only a kind of make-believe mother that certain men feel they need. Such an experiment works best at a great distance. Edgar loved only me. Korbowski knows something about it.

WATER HEN Mr. Korbowski may know a great deal, but in matters of feelings of the sort that united me with Duke Edgar, he simply isn't competent to judge.

LADY You're just a phantom. An imagined value. I'm not at all jealous of you. I prefer reality to your spiritual seductions in the fourth dimension. Edgar told me that he wrote you nonsensical letters which you took seriously. It's all ridiculous and petty.

WATER HEN That's not true.

KORBOWSKI The Duke told me so just before he died; he was reading that big fat book full of symbols and expiring at the same time.

LADY Yes, he was reading Russell and Whitehead's *Principia Mathematica* after his entrails had been torn out by a tiger. He was a hero. He was fully conscious when he said he'd duped you into a metaphysical flirtation. He called it the psychopaths' metaphysical flirtation. Yet he wasn't a madman himself.

WATER HEN (*bursts out laughing suddenly*) · Ha, ha, ha! I was the one who was pulling his leg. I lie about everything. I don't exist at all. I live only by lying. Is there anything more sublime than lying for its own sake? Read those letters. That man believed in me, but he had moments of horrible despair and tried to convince himself that he was the one who was lying. In that lay the drama of his life. That's why he was so brave. I was the one who didn't want to meet him.

LADY Yes, because he would have been disillusioned. He didn't even have a photo of you; you wanted to be something in the nature of a myth. That's why you never have your picture taken. Everybody knows all about that. (*The Hen wants to say something in answer.*)

TADZIO (*jumps up*) Take that woman away. I don't want her here. She tells lies. (*He stamps his foot.*)

EDGAR (*in a weak voice*) Tadzio, don't—behave yourself!

LADY Jan, show that woman out this instant. (*Jan, who up until now has stood erect near Edgar's head, moves toward the Hen.*)

FATHER I'll escort her to the door myself. Elizabeth, give me your hand. In your own way you are great. (*They go toward the door hand in hand. Tadzio sits down at Edgar's feet.*)

EDGAR (*still lying down*) So you're against me too, Father?

FATHER (*turning around at the door*) Not against you, but with you against life. I'm waiting for you to finally become an artist.

EDGAR (*still lying down*) Alice, save me from him; save me from myself. (*He notices Korbowski standing irresolutely with the letters in his hand.*) Out, scum! Out!

KORBOWSKI (*bowing humbly; to the Lady*) And the letters?

LADY You may take them with you, Mr. Korbowski. Reading that correspondence will be good for your psyche; you'll be more mixed up than ever. Please go right ahead. (*She points to the door on the right. Afrosia sits down in the armchair to the left. Korbowski hesitates.*) Jan! (*Jan shoves Korbowski gently toward the door. Korbowski scarcely resists.*)

JAN All right, Tom, none of your tricks. (*They go off to the right.*)

TYPOWICZ (*pulls some papers out of his side pocket and goes over to Edgar*) Mr. Valpor, as guardian of your wife's estate, will you please sign here. We've drawn up the final version of the charter of the Theosophical Jam Company. (*He gives him a fountain pen. Edgar signs lying down.*)

EDGAR And now, gentlemen, forgive me, but I can't go on. (*The three old men bow, kiss Alice's hand, and leave.*) Alice, I beg you, let's start a new life.

LADY (*with a smile*) Not another one, but a new one?

EDGAR That was impossible . . . (*He looks at Tadzio as if he had not noticed him before.*) Tadzio, go to bed this minute!

TADZIO (*getting up*) But won't you believe me now? I believe in you, my dear, dear Papa. I woke up when that woman said she didn't want to be my mother. I want to be good.

LADY I want to be good, too.

EDGAR (*paying no attention to what she has said, to Tadzio*) How will wanting to be good help, if there's evil in the very depths of your soul? Besides, I must admit I've gone beyond such categories today. Ethics is only the consequence of a large number of individuals thinking the same way. A man on a desert island wouldn't have any notion of what it means. Tadzio, go to bed.

TADZIO But won't you believe me, Papa? I'm not talking about you, Mama; you have double eyes. Now I know why you're my father.

EDGAR I want to believe you, just as you want to be good. (*He kisses him on the forehead.*) (*Without saying good-bye to the Lady, Tadzio goes slowly to the left, his head lowered. Afrosia gets up and follows him.*)

LADY (*sitting down beside Edgar on the small couch*) Do you really feel as though you were on a desert island?

EDGAR Save me, Alice. I'm tired of being a superman. The temptation of penance was too much for me. Father's against me, and so is Elizabeth. Together the two of them tempt me. (*He speaks feverishly.*) There's an even worse temptation waiting for me—he inoculated me with it: the temptation to become an artist. I'm defending myself with what little strength I have left. I have no talent, I'm great in my utter nothingness. Today life has lost all meaning.

LADY Just because that liar walked out on you?

EDGAR (*still more feverishly*) No, no. This suffering . . . I don't even want to talk about it. I can't describe it. Rescue me from Art; I hate Art, and I'm afraid of it. Now that life has lost its meaning, that other temptation's becoming stronger and stronger. I won't be able to resist it unless you protect me. Alice, I hardly dare ask you; all my bones ache after those tortures. For once, kiss me as if you really loved me.

LADY (*bending over him*) I feel that I really do love you now. (*She kisses him on the lips. A long kiss.*)

EDGAR (*pushing her away*) But it's all petty, petty, petty.

LADY (*getting up and stretching*) Only in lying is there greatness.

EDGAR (*raising himself up a little*) Oh, so you're against me, too? Life awaits us in all its horror.

LADY (*slowly, emphatically*) I won't leave you. Neither you nor Tadzio.

EDGAR Like condemned prisoners we'll drag on and on until death.

ACT III

The same room as in Act II. Evening. The chandelier is lighted. Ten years have elapsed. A suite of furniture stands on the right-hand side of

*the stage. A small couch covered in something green on the left. On the
right, by the door, a small folded card table. Tadzio, as a young man
twenty years old, sits lost in thought in an armchair on the left. He is
dressed in a gray suit. Suddenly he begins nervously to tap his right
foot against the floor.*

TADZIO When will this ghastly nightmare ever end? It's just like a life
sentence. God knows what father expects of me; he's a failure
himself. What a fine example! (*Gets up*) For the time being I'll
listen dutifully. But as soon as it all blows up, I won't have to look
up to anybody. Korbowski—there was a man. What a pity he wasn't
my father! (*Walking up and down*) You forget everything—even
that women exist! Mathematics, mathematics! It's a hell of a life!
(*Knocking at the door to the right. Jan enters.*)

JAN Sir, the lady who was here ten years ago wishes to speak to you.

TADZIO What? (*Remembers*) Oh! Show her in. Hurry up. I behaved so
badly then. (*He goes to the door. The Water Hen enters, dressed as
in Act II, but she wears a black cape and a black hat, something in
the style of Napoleon's "en bataille," and an orange sweater. She has
not aged at all. On the contrary, she is very seductive. Her eyes seem
more slanted and her lips redder. Her whole face is lighted up with
sensuality, of which there was no trace in Acts I and II. Her hair is
cut short and is curled.*)

WATER HEN Are you Mr. Tadeusz Valpor?

TADEUSZ (*flustered*) Yes, I am. In the old days we both had the same
name.

WATER HEN I know that. A pure coincidence. That's why people
suspected I was your mother. You were the one who desperately
wanted me to be your mother, and you got offended when I refused.
Ha, ha. What a ridiculous rumor! Don't you agree? (*Jan leaves
smiling.*)

TADEUSZ (*still more flustered*) I was a child then. But please—do sit
down. (*The Hen sits down in the armchair to the left where he had
been sitting; Tadeusz near her, his left profile to the audience.*) But
you look even younger now, as far as I can remember from the old
days.

WATER HEN (*greatly flustered*) Yes . . . It's Indian yoga, plus American massage. Ludicrous, isn't it? Ha, ha! (*She conceals her embar-
rassment by laughing. She laughs "till her sides split," loudly. Tadeusz is grimly flustered. It is evident that the Hen is making one hell
of an erotic impression on him.*)

TADEUSZ (*sullenly*) Properly speaking, why are you laughing?

WATER HEN (*pulling herself together*) Properly speaking, I'm laughing quite improperly. And what are you doing these days? (*With an ironic stress on* you.)

TADEUSZ Me? I'm not doing anything. I study. Mathematics. They torture me with mathematics, even though I don't have any talent for it.

WATER HEN That runs in your family. Your grandfather was dead set on making an artist out of your father. So far as I know, it was a complete failure.

TADEUSZ That's true, as of now. Although it's still a subject of endless controversy. (*Returning to the original topic*) You know, what I'm going to say may sound absurd: I'm so busy that I sometimes forget women exist. Yesterday as I was going to class, I caught sight of a good-looking woman, and I swear for a minute I didn't know what sort of a creature I was looking at. Then I realized that there are such things as women, and I was deliriously happy. (*He breaks off and becomes embarrassed; the Water Hen has become gloomy.*) What I'm saying is all nonsense. Maybe it seems very childish to you, but . . .

WATER HEN (*takes off her hat and puts it on the table; she tosses her cape back on the arm of the chair; her face brightens*) Well, and what else?

TADEUSZ Nothing. You said there was something that runs in our family. But you know that I'm only my father's adopted son.

WATER HEN (*flustered*) Yes, I know.

TADEUSZ But sometimes I could swear that it was you who first called him my father. I was very ill then—that's for certain.

WATER HEN (*she suddenly moves a little closer to him and asks with sudden shamelessness*): Do I appeal to you?

TADEUSZ (*he is momentarily, as they say, "thunderstruck"; suddenly he takes a deep breath and speaks in a choked voice*) I like you tremendously. I love you. (*He throws himself at her. She pushes him away, laughing.*)

WATER HEN Just like that, "I love you." And what about that woman in the street? When all of a sudden you remembered that women exist.

TADEUSZ That was nothing. I love only you. Let me kiss you . . . (*He kisses her on the lips violently. The Hen yields.*)

WATER HEN (*pushing him away*) That's enough . . . Someone's coming.

TADEUSZ (*out of his mind*) Tell me you love me. I've just kissed you for the first time. It's tremendous. Tell me you love me.

WATER HEN (*kisses him violently*) I love you—you innocent little thing. You'll be my . . .

(*Enter Father and Edgar. They stand on the threshold astounded. Tadeusz jumps away from the Hen. The Father clean-shaven, but much older. Edgar, who has aged a great deal, looks over fifty; both are dressed in the same way, like Tadeusz.*)

FATHER Here's a new development! (*He recognizes the Hen; Edgar stands by the door absorbed; Tadeusz, flustered, to the left.*) Good evening, Elizabeth. (*The Hen gets up.*) I haven't seen you for ages! You're quite the coquette now, aren't you! (*To Tadeusz*) Well, you rascal, playing footsie with her already, eh?

TADEUSZ I love this woman, and I intend to marry her. I've awakened from my dream again. Now I know what it all means and what all of you wanted from me. Nothing doing. I don't want to be that kind of person. I don't accept any of these new theories!

WATER HEN (*taking his arm*) He's mine. He's suffocating here with all of you. He's handsome. He has a beautiful soul. He'll become great through me.

EDGAR (*coming up to her, angry*) All of a sudden he's got a beautiful soul and greatness too just because you find him attractive. You don't know him. And you'll probably make him great the way you wanted to make me great. It's all petty, disgustingly petty.

FATHER Greatness has gone to your heads. In my time at least it was possible to become a great artist. But now even that doesn't work . . .

WATER HEN (*not paying attention to him*) You two want to warp his life the way I warped yours. (*She points to herself and to Edgar in a certain crude way.*)

FATHER You warped my cat's life too, Elizabeth, by feeding him lemons. But the cat died, and in this case we've got to go on living, or else we'd better blow our brains out right away.

EDGAR That's just it. I won't let you use Tadeusz for your suicidal experiments or for your artificial crimes. He'll be a scholar. The only profession in the world that hasn't already gone to the dogs or to some still worse creatures.

TADEUSZ I don't want to be a scholar at all. I love Miss Elizabeth.

EDGAR You think that'll satisfy you? You're not a woman, that won't fill your life. Look at him; he's invented a new career: being in love! A third-rate Don Juan—what am I saying?—a common Juan without the Don.

WATER HEN He knows intuitively who he is. You two can distort anything. If you won't let a criminal be a criminal, he'll become something still worse—a fake, a fraud. Father, you're the one who's contaminating everyone with your programs.

EDGAR Since when have you repudiated lying? A long time ago? Or is this a new lie especially created for the present situation?

WATER HEN There's no truth in words or in any actions or professions men devise. Truth is what is actually happening.

EDGAR Look here, what sort of real-life dadaism is that? Do as the apes do, live in trees! But I'm going to remind you once more of that other time. (*To his Father*) Father, talk with them. I'll be right back. (*He leaves, almost running, to the left.*)

FATHER Well, what do you say about that, youngsters?

TADEUSZ Nothing. Either Father lets me marry this woman, or I'll run away from home. That's final.

FATHER I have nothing more to say to you. I'll watch what happens as a spectator.

(*The Lady enters from the left side of the stage, dressed in an azure dressing gown trimmed in lace. She is very well-preserved, but slightly made up.*)

LADY Oh, it's you. New revelations about my first husband perhaps?

WATER HEN That topic doesn't concern me any more. I've destroyed the past completely.

LADY (*coming up to her and speaking with venom*) But you haven't destroyed yourself in the process, have you? You look very pretty. I realized at once that something was going on when Edgar rushed in like a lunatic racing against time and changed into his eighteenth-century outfit. Apparently he wants to entice you with the past.

WATER HEN It won't work. I love Tadeusz. He's going to marry me.

LADY So soon? (*To Tadeusz*) Tadzio, is that true?

TADEUSZ (*in a hard tone of voice*) Yes. I've finally awakened from my dream and seen through all your lies. Manufacturing artificial people, artificial crimes, artificial penance, artificial everything.

LADY This one is always waking up from some dream or other and beginning to understand everything. How many times now have you come to understand everything? What's the grand total?

TADEUSZ I've understood twice. But everything is infinite, there's no point in talking about actual quantities of anything. When I understand for the third time, it may very well be the end. (*The Hen nestles close to him in silence.*)

LADY A regular little Solomon. Watch out you don't tempt fate by talking about that third time. Watch out! (*She shakes her finger at him. Jan enters from the right.*)

JAN Tom Hoozy, Your Grace.

LADY Hoozy?

JAN *False* de Korbowa-Korbowski, Your Grace.

LADY (*amazed*) I didn't know that was his real name. Ask Mr. Hoozy to come in. (*Exit Jan.*)

FATHER Here's a new complication. Undoubtedly he knew all about it. Life holds no interest for me any more.

    (*Korbowski enters, dressed in a threadbare sports coat, sports cap, a thick walking stick in his hand. His face is ravaged and aged, but handsome. He looks more noble than before.*)

LADY Mr. Korbowski, *recte* Hoozy, sit down and be a silent witness to events. (*Korbowski bows and sits in the armchair to the right. At this moment Edgar runs in, dressed in the costume he wore in Act I, with a hat.*)

WATER HEN What kind of a masquerade is this? Ham. He's changed into his old costume to create an atmosphere. Too bad you didn't dress up as a Mexican general or Julius Caesar.

TADEUSZ Really, Papa, that's too much, you're making a farce of a very serious situation.

EDGAR Silence. I forbid you to marry that person.

KORBOWSKI (*gets up*) Mr. Valpor, please wait a minute. I apologize for being here, but I've been authorized by the Duchess. I still love her. For the last five years I've been observing your life together. I spent five years in the Argentine.

EDGAR What's that to me? Get to the point.

KORBOWSKI As soon as that witch appeared, I knew that today would be the crucial day. (*Points to the Hen*) The police are on my track, but since I was a former witness, I took the chance and came to help you. Besides, there's a revolution going on, and I mean to come out on top. If everything comes crashing down today, I'll have nothing to fear.

EDGAR (*who has been listening impatiently*) That will do, you can finish later. Tadzio, today you're at the turning point of your life. If you insist on staying with that woman, you're lost.

TADEUSZ That's because you're sweet on her yourself, Father. The proof is that you've changed your clothes. You overdo everything.

EDGAR Tadzio, I'm telling you for the last time. I love you, but my patience . . .

TADEUSZ (*interrupts him brutally*) Father, you're an old ham, and besides you're not my father at all. Don't forget that while I'm talking to you, Father, I'm wide awake, not dreaming.

EDGAR (*petrified, he roars*) You scoundrel!

TADEUSZ Yes, I'm a scoundrel . . .

EDGAR Shut up! Shut up! (*Throws himself at Tadzio and tears him away from the Hen*) You won't marry her. I won't let you.

TADEUSZ If that's the case, I'm leaving the house right now and you'll never see me again. Understand, Father? Not another word.

KORBOWSKI (*to Edgar*) Mr. Valpor, come to your senses. First of all, we've got to kill this slut. (*Mysteriously to the Lady*) Follow my game, Alice? (*To Edgar*) It's the only way out, Mr. Valpor.

EDGAR Yes, you're right, Mr. Korbowski. I'm glad you've come. Thank you. (*Shouts*) Jan! Jan! (*Jan appears in the door to the right.*) My double-barreled shotgun, a bullet in each barrel! (*Jan disappears.*)

WATER HEN That's enough play-acting. Tadeusz, we're leaving right now. I can't stand petty lying.

EDGAR This is no lie, I'm not joking. (*The Lamplighter enters.*)

LAMPLIGHTER The lantern has been lit.

EDGAR What lantern? Who are you? (*The cherry-colored curtain is drawn back, and between the columns appears the landscape from Act I with the pole and lighted lantern. The mound is not visible behind the stairs.*)

LAMPLIGHTER Playing dumb! As though you'd just dropped in out of the blue! Look over there! (*He points out the landscape. Everybody looks in that direction.*)

EDGAR Oh, that! I'd forgotten. Thank you, my good man, you may go now. (*He gives him a tip. The Lamplighter goes away muttering something unintelligible. At the door he meets Jan carrying the gun.*)

JAN It's loaded, sir. (*Everybody turns around. Edgar takes the gun.*)

WATER HEN (*to Tadeusz*) Are you coming or not?

TADEUSZ (*he gives a start, as if awakened from a dream, and speaks in a daze*) I'm coming.

EDGAR Not one step! (*To the Hen*) Stand over there. (*He points to the stairs.*)

WATER HEN I wouldn't dream of it. I'm sick of your idiotic jokes.

EDGAR Jan, get that woman and hold her. I'm going to shoot her.

JAN Sir, I'm afraid you just might shoot me too.

EDGAR Hold that woman, I said. (*The Hen makes a movement toward the door.*)

JAN Please stop joking, sir.

EDGAR You blockhead, you know I'm an excellent shot. *Tir aux pigeons* —first prize. Take her and put her on target, or I'll shoot you dead as a dog without a moment's hesitation. (*He says the last words in a threatening tone. Jan grabs her and drags her to the left toward the stairs.*)

WATER HEN I've had enough of these idiotic jokes. Let go of me, you boor. Edgar, have you really gone mad? (*Jan drags her onto the stairs. They stand against the background of the landscape. Tadeusz has raised his hands to his head in incredulous horror. He stands petrified. Lady and Father, craning their necks this way and that, look first at Edgar and then at the group on the stairs, with horrified curiosity.*)

EDGAR (*to Jan*) Hold her still. (*He aims.*)

WATER HEN (*shouts*) Edgar, I love you, only you. I was only trying to make you jealous.

EDGAR (*coldly*) Too late!

WATER HEN He's a madman, he already shot me once. Save me! (*Edgar aims, moving the barrel to follow the Hen's movements as she struggles to tear herself away. Two shots are fired. Jan lets go of the Hen, and she falls down on the threshold between the columns.*)

JAN (*bending over her*) Her head's split wide open! (*coming down*) You sure are a whale of a madman! Damned if you're not! (*He scratches his head admiringly.*)

EDGAR (*calmly*) It all happened once before, only a little differently. (*To Jan*) Take this. (*Jan takes the shotgun and exits. At the door he passes the three detectives whom no one sees.*)

TADEUSZ Now I've finally awakened from my third dream. I know everything now. I'm an unmitigated scoundrel.

EDGAR Serves you right. I hate you. I haven't even got an adopted son. I'm all alone. (*Remembering*) What about you, Alice?

LADY (*pointing to the door*) Look over there, look over there. (*Two detectives throw themselves on Korbowski and pin his arms back. The curtain is drawn shut.*)

ORSIN My apologies, ladies and gentlemen. But we've been tipped off that Tom Hoozy, one of the most dangerous criminals in the world, just came in here.

LADY Richard, I've been the cause of your undoing. I left you for that idiot. (*She points to Edgar.*)

KORBOWSKI (*held by the detectives*) It doesn't matter. There's a revolution going on. We'll meet again. This won't last long. Perhaps today we'll all be free. Alice, I loved you and you only even in the thick of crimes so monstrous as to be four-dimensional and non-Euclidean in their swinishness. (*The Lady wants to go over to him.*)

ORSIN (*noticing the Hen's body*) Stay where you are. Who's that lying over there? (*He points to the stairs. Edgar makes a gesture, as though he wanted to say something.*)

LADY (*quickly*) I killed that woman, because she was in love with him. (*She points to Korbowski, who smiles blissfully. Tadeusz, taking advantage of the confusion, sneaks away to the left toward the door. Edgar stands still. Father, completely bewildered, is silent.*)

ORSIN Quite a cosy little nest! Madam—I mean, Duchess Nevermore—
ho, ho—*secundo voto* * Valpor—so this is how you operate? (*Tadeusz flees impetuously through the door on the right. Orsin flings
himself after him. Tadeusz escapes.*)

KORBOWSKI (*shouting after him*) Don't worry, we'll meet again. (*To
the Lady*) Don't you understand, Alice, now he's really turned into
a hopeless scoundrel. And in times like these he may be destined to
play a great role. (*Jan pulls the Hen's body to the other side of the
curtain.*)

ORSIN That's enough talk. Take them both to prison. (*Sounds like the
pounding of feet, confused singing and shouting can be heard in the
street.*)

FIRST DETECTIVE I don't know if we'll make it, things are starting to get
hot out there.

ORSIN We'd better hurry. (*Two shots are heard, followed by a burst of
machine-gun fire.*)

KORBOWSKI It's going nicely. Let's go out into the streets. I like the
atmosphere of a revolution. There's nothing more agreeable than to
swim in the black sea of a mob gone mad. (*The din offstage
continues.*)

LADY Richard, I love and admire you. Can there be any greater happiness than not to despise the man one loves?
     (*The detectives lead Korbowski out. Alice follows him; Orsin
follows them.*)

LADY (*passing across the stage*) Good-bye, Father. I'm leaving the
house and the money to you. (*She leaves without looking at
Edgar.*)

FATHER Well, Sonny, now what? We've gone bankrupt. All we need
now is for Tadzio to turn out to be Korbowski's son. But we'll never
know about that. Perhaps now you'll become an artist. You could
even become an actor; after all, actors are now creative artists too,
ever since Pure Form became all the rage. (*Edgar stands silently; the
noise offstage becomes louder and louder; bursts of machine-gun
fire.*) Well, make up your mind! Surely nothing ties you to life any
more? Now you've got to become an artist.

EDGAR Death still ties me to life. That's the last thing to be disposed
of.

FATHER How?

EDGAR (*pulls a revolver out of his pocket*) Like this. (*He shows it to
his father.*)

---

* Latin, "according to vow," i.e., by marriage. [Translators' note]

FATHER You'd be an excellent actor, especially in those preposterous plays they write nowadays. But why did you use a shotgun when you had a revolver? So it would be more difficult to figure out? Huh?

EDGAR Because I wanted it to be the same as before.

FATHER I've always said you were an artist. Everything's neatly worked out in prepared speeches. You could write plays. Come here, let me give you a hug.

EDGAR Later, I don't have time now. Good-bye, Father. (*He shoots himself in the right temple and falls to the ground. Father stands goggle-eyed for a moment.*)

FATHER (*affectedly*) "Oh, thus the artist dies"—without any self-knowledge. Not like that other ham. (*He shouts*) Jan! Jan! (*Jan runs in.*) The young master has killed himself. Call the albinos, have them carry him out.

JAN I always thought it would turn out this way. (*He bends down over the corpse.*) It was a perfect shot. A tiny little hole like a nail makes. (*The noise in the street reaches its peak.*) What a shot that guy was! But he sure gave me a good scare today!

FATHER Jan, open the door, they're beating on it. The mob must be tearing everything down. (*Jan goes out.*) It's strange how old age and sea duty blunt everything in a man. I honestly don't feel anything at all—either for good or evil. Damn it all, a man isn't a ship! (*Enter Typowicz, Evader, and Specter.*) At last! (*To the old men*) My son killed himself. His nerves got the better of him. Too bad. Well, what's going on out there?

TYPOWICZ (*pale, the others frightfully dejected*) Mr. Valpor, cheer up. Everything's going to the devil. The Semites will always find a way. There are heaps of corpses out there in the street. We came on foot. Our chauffeur ran away. They took our car. We saw a strange sight. The Duchess was walking along the street in her dressing gown with Korbowski; some thugs were holding them prisoner. We couldn't get near them. (*The albinos come in and take Edgar's body out.*) Korbowski kept shouting something. Then the mob beat the thugs to a pulp, and Korbowski and the Duchess went off with the crowd to the barricade near Angry Young Man Avenue. But what am I saying? It's all a dream! Our company no longer exists. The new government has abolished all private enterprise. All we have left is what we've got abroad in foreign banks. (*During this speech, the albinos carry out Edgar's body to the left.*) And what about our homes?

EVADER They're community property too. We've lost everything.

FATHER I wonder if my adopted grandson will fight his way to the top.

(*Suddenly*) Well, gentlemen, it's our last night; the gangsters will probably butcher us tomorrow, so let's amuse ourselves for the last time. (*Shouts*) Jan! (*Jan in the doorway*) Set up the card table. (*Jan throws himself forward and with incredible speed sets up the card table in the middle of the room.*)

EVADER Have you gone out of your mind? To play cards at such a critical time?

FATHER At our age it's the only way of whiling away the time during a social upheaval. What else could we do? Whist or auction bridge? "That is the question." *

TYPOWICZ Why not whist? (*Burst of machine-gun fire*)

FATHER Oh, did you hear that? How could we do anything else except play cards? Everything's falling to pieces anyway.

SPECTER It would seem that you're right.

FATHER Of course. Jan, cold supper *extra fin* and plenty of wine for all. We'll drink like dragons. We've got to drink away three abortive generations. Maybe I'll still become a revolutionary admiral, but those others—ugh—what a comedown! (*Typowicz, Specter, and Evader sit down at the table, leaving a place facing the audience for Father. Typowicz with his back to the audience, Evader on the left, Specter to the right. Faint bursts of machine-gun fire and a distant roar of heavy artillery shells exploding.*)

FATHER (*to Jan who stands in the doorway*) Jan, one thing more. Go get those girls to keep us company at dinner, you know—the ones the young master and I used to visit.

JAN But will they want to come when all hell's breaking loose?

FATHER Certainly they'll want to, promise them anything. (*Exit Jan; Father goes over to the table and inspects the cards.*) There's no need to worry, gentlemen, perhaps we can still get jobs in the new government.

TYPOWICZ One club.

EVADER Two clubs.

FATHER (*sitting down*) Two diamonds. (*A red glare floods the stage, and the monstrous boom of a grenade exploding nearby can be heard.*) Banging away in fine style. Your bid, Mr. Specter.

SPECTER (*in a quivering, somewhat plaintive voice*) Two hearts. The world is collapsing. (*Fainter red flashes of lighting, and immediately afterward two shells exploding a little farther off*)

TYPOWICZ Pass.

_____
* In English in the original. [Translators' note]

The Crazy Locomotive

INTRODUCTION

The Crazy Locomotive (*Szalona locomotywa*, 1923) is unique among Witkiewicz' dramas in that it confronts the challenge of mechanization directly. In this appropriately short, violent play, Witkiewicz puts the machine on the stage, turns it on, and lets us see where it will lead. The machine is a self-destructive machine—it blows itself up.

Witkiewicz utilizes the mechanized techniques of the enemy to subvert and destroy mechanization. The machine, simultaneously exploited and attacked, is both the locomotive engine and the movie projector. *The Crazy Locomotive* is a superparody—of the worship of the machine and of the new arts of technology: futurism and cinema. By his ironic appropriation of their ideas and devices, Witkiewicz was able to create an antifuturistic, anticinematographic play that has all the metallic brilliance and frantic speed which he is mocking.

Witkiewicz knew the futurists and their work from the Paris exhibition in February, 1912. He refers to Gino Severini in *They*, calling him "Severin." From the various manifestos published in many different languages at the time of the exhibition, Witkiewicz would have been acquainted with the principal ideas of the futurists: worship of action for its own sake; glorification of war, violence, and speed; love of physical courage and daring in the face of danger; and preference for the machine in motion as the new ideal of beauty. In the Preface to the *Initial Manifesto of Futurism*, Marinetti sees himself "alone with the black phantoms that rummage about in the red-hot bellies of the locomotives launched at furious speeds," [1] and in the Manifesto itself, he states:

> We declare that the world's splendor has been enriched by a new beauty; the beauty of speed. . . . We shall sing of the man at the steering wheel, whose ideal stem transfixes the Earth, rushing over the circuit of her orbit. . . . Why should we look behind us, when we have to break in the mysterious portals of the Impossible? Time and Space died yesterday. Already we live in the absolute, since we have already created speed, eternal and ever-present. . . . We shall sing . . . of

---

[1] Filippo Tommaso Marinetti, "Preface to the Initial Manifesto of Futurism," in Raffaele Carrieri, *Futurism* (Milan: Edizioni del Milione, 1963), p. 11.

broadchested locomotives prancing on the rails, like huge steel horses bridled with long tubes. . . .[2]

The futurist hero was to be a mechanized superman: "the disciple of the Engine, the enemy of books, an exponent of personal experience."[3] He should act savagely and instinctively. "We are immoral, destroyers, disorganizers; we want death and madness."[4] The futurists celebrated the motorized masses who would ultimately be transformed into machines through the impact of metal and speed, "when the Animal Kingdom comes to its end and the Mechanical Realm begins."[5]

In Act I of *The Crazy Locomotive* two social and psychological outlaws, Tréfaldi and Travaillac, masquerading as the locomotive engineer Tenser and his fireman Slobok, embark on a desperate metaphysical adventure in search of the Absolute. The metallic beast roars through artificial landscapes, annihilating time and space. Speed becomes the principle and criterion of all things. Through sheer acceleration the characters aboard the engine-island hope to escape from the confines of everyday life and the boredom of existence and find a meaning to fill the void. Traveling at breakneck speed, Tréfaldi and Travaillac immediately experience a sense of elation and freedom denied them on firm ground. Their journey along the rails turns inward and becomes a journey into the mind, a retreat from the world and a return to wonderful memories of childhood. "We're on our desert island again: Robinson Crusoe and his man Friday. We're playing the Robinson game the way we did when we were children," Tréfaldi tells Travaillac.

Robinson Crusoe and Friday, engineer and fireman, master and servant, aristocrat and proletarian—the two criminals are contrasting types with different physical traits, personalities, and social backgrounds. Prince Tréfaldi is refined, highly educated, impractical, and by nature philosophical; his face is long and lean, his beard and mustache elegant. Travaillac (whose name comes from the French *travailler*, "to work") is crude, uneducated, wary, and by nature a doer; his features are coarse, his face clean-shaven. Tréfaldi has an aristocratic aloofness about him and is free from class consciousness and sexual jealousy; Travaillac is direct in his responses and shows considerable jealousy over Julia and awareness of his social position in relation to his boss. What unites them is the past and the future:

[2] Marinetti, "Initial Manifesto of Futurism," in Joshua C. Taylor, *Futurism* (New York: Museum of Modern Art, 1961), p. 124.

[3] Marinetti, quoted by Rosa Trillo Clough, *Futurism* (New York: Philosophical Library, 1961), p. 33.

[4] Giulio Evola, "Notes for Friends," in *After Boccioni* (Rome: Edizioni Mediterranee; Studio d'Arte Contemporanea "La Medusa," 1961), p. 35.

[5] Marinetti, quoted by Clough, *Futurism*, p. 41.

memories of their former criminal glories, and hopes for a new life of liberation and excitement.

Their complementary personalities and the games they play in their isolation in a self-contained world suggest the interplay between Estragon and Vladimir in Samuel Beckett's *Waiting for Godot*,[6] but the comparison only serves to show the fundamental difference between the two pairs of characters and the two plays. Witkiewicz' absurd duo are willful participants in a soul-shattering adventure. Even though the initiative rests primarily with Tréfaldi, both the engineer and his fireman are actively pursuing a goal rather than waiting passively for something to happen.

The characters abound in energy that parallels the driving force of the engine; as the locomotive speeds up, it releases the deepest and darkest forces normally hidden within the subconscious recesses of their personalities and permits them to break through into frenzied action. Minna's uncontrollable passion for Travaillac and Julia's ecstasy in being in love with both Tréfaldi and Travaillac are other manifestations of the same subliminal urges; like the frantic speed and the feverish talk, sexual attraction is an irrational, elemental plunge beyond all the bounds of society and the normal laws of conduct.

Extraordinary hopes are raised in Act I. As Tréfaldi and Travaillac reach a progressively closer intellectual rapport, the speed of the locomotive increases. They not only hope to experience a superreality; they are actually creating it themselves by their actions. Julia identifies opening the throttle all the way with her falling in love with both of them and also with the act of primeval creation. "Something's being created right here and now, the way it was in the beginning before the world began."

But in Act II the prophecy of a new birth begins to ring false. Instead of the creation of a new world, there will be only the destruction of an old one. As a machine, the locomotive must follow along the rails, and where they lead is known in advance—to a predictable, mechanized disaster. Tréfaldi is starting to become the slave of the beast which he let loose to liberate him. "I'm only an extension of this throttle," he complains, "as if my brains had been skewered and spitted on this iron lever. But it's more than that; I've become the engine." His hand on the throttle is no longer controlled by his mind; it has become part of the machine. As he wonders whether mechanized madness will eventually swallow up the whole world, he feels his personality being drained of all its energy; his head is empty, and he is powerless to stop acting as a part of a piece of machinery in which he no longer believes.

[6] Martin Esslin, *The Theater of the Absurd* (New York: Anchor Books, Doubleday and Co. 1961), p. 15.

The Epilogue shows the consequences of flight to a higher reality via a machine: death and madness. Tréfaldi—Marinetti's "man at the steering wheel"—ends up with the steering wheel twelve inches through his guts, with appropriate irony since he had wanted to live by guts alone, rather than according to his intellect. He was skewered by the instrument of control, not in his brain as he had imagined before, but in the seat of his intuition, instinct, and daring. Julia's former ecstasy has turned into madness and despair as she confronts the catastrophe in an uncomprehending state of shock. The primordial elements that were to be shaped into the great new creation have gone back to chaos and slime: the spilled guts, mushlike brains, and confused groans and cries that fill the stage. The wonderful metallic animal itself bursts into fragments; all that is left is a heap of debris.

With the introduction of the mad wife of the railway guard in the very last minutes of the play, Witkiewicz throws the whole spectral quality of the Epilogue into a new dimension of moonlight and insanity. Decked out in flowers like the mad Ophelia, Jeanne claims to have waited for such a disaster all her life. In the night a spirit with cat's eyes appeared to her in a dream, made love to her, and told her to cut the telephone wires. She points to Tréfaldi as her demon lover. Madness and dream, a collective daze and a landscape of subconscious fears and desires—this is the "black abyss" that suddenly opens before us in the Epilogue. Life is the shadow of a dream. The cold, cruel futuristic "joy ride" plunges into the void.

Jeanne's sudden, frightening appearance at the end of *The Crazy Locomotive* is an example of one of the characteristic masterstrokes of Witkiewicz' dramaturgy: his daring use of a minor character as a catalyst to open the abyss at the very denouement. The playwright is able to give strange and sinister weight to these messengers from another realm who, even though they have only a speech or two and most often are appearing on stage for the first time, act as the voice of doom. Unlike their ancestors in Greek drama, Witkiewicz' messengers do not report on the off-stage actions of the heroes and gods—they come from another world and remind the heroes of its existence and their relation to it. The ominous appearances of the Lamplighter in *The Water Hen* and of Professor Walldorff in *The Madman and the Nun* function similarly. These ghastly arrivals are unpredictable and therefore startling and theatrical, but once they have taken place they seem appropriate and inevitable—exactly the effect that Witkiewicz felt Pure Form should produce.

Dr. Marcellus Riftmaker, on the other hand, is the efficient man of science, standing outside the world of madness and coming to restore order. His prime interest is in saving Tréfaldi so that he can be punished as an example to others. "Justice first, then the wounded, and the mentally ill last of all." He is another kind of machine, the disciplinary social automationist with rigid categories and systems, and no sympathy for human weakness.

In addition to wrecking the futurist machine, *The Crazy Locomotive* collides head-on with the cinema. Witkiewicz' attitude toward the film was hostile; he saw it as a deadly challenge to the art of the theater. In *Aesthetic Sketches,* published in 1922, the year before Witkiewicz wrote *The Crazy Locomotive,* in the chapter devoted to "The Decline of Art," he poses the question of the very survival of the theater:

> With cinematography you can do absolutely anything you want, so is it worth trying to preserve idle chatter on the stage, which nobody needs anyhow, when you can have such frantic action and such violent images instead; is it worth making the effort to produce something as devilishly difficult as a real play for the theater faced with a rival as dangerous as the all-powerful cinema?

In *The Crazy Locomotive* Witkiewicz accepts the challenge and proves that the stage can present frantic action and violent images, as well as the intellectual content or "idle chatter," incorporating the film within the play and thereby deliberately calling attention to the unreal nature of this play-within-the-play. The entire play is a parody of the stereotypes of early films.

The headlong race of the crazy locomotive is itself probably inspired by famous train chases like Abel Gance's *La Roue* (1922), in which the central character is the engineer and the denouement a train wreck. The element of parody is reinforced by the actual use of film for the moving landscape and ironically commented upon by remarks such as Julia's exclamation: "I've always dreamed of something really extraordinary happening to me, like in the movies!" The double identities of Tréfaldi and Travaillac juxtapose the world of illusion and fantasy with the prosaic everyday world which they are trying to escape. Their colorful cinematographic careers as kings of the underworld are an externalization of the dreams and longings of the other passengers in the rear cars.

> TRAVAILLAC: But just think: here we are talking about all this, and back there, in one of the cars on the train, someone's reading about the very same thing, a story just like ours, in a murder mystery from the lending library.

But is the cheap fiction a parody of their lives, or are they a parody of the cheap fiction? Travaillac's speech ironically reminds the audience of the other world from which the two metaphysical adventurers think they have been freed. But there is no possibility of leaving firm ground, and soon the farcical world of cheap fiction readers—bureaucrats, thugs, and policemen—comes crawling up into the locomotive, invading the intense isolation of the questers and degrading their mission with the slapstick scuffle that follows. The fight aboard the moving train between the outlaws and the bumbling law-enforcement officials, as the passengers (representing a cross section of society) watch in outrage and horror, is cinematographic parody in another key.

The philosophical discussion between Tréfaldi and Travaillac, carried on against the ever increasing speed of the locomotive, is an attempt by men who belong to an earlier age to resolve fundamental problems through argumentation and rhetoric. It is a losing battle: philosophical dialogue versus uncontrollable movement. Cinema wins, dialogue ceases. Revolver shots, blows on the head with a shovel, a violent clang, a terrible crash finally drown out all words. The counterpoint and alternation of prolonged discussion and sudden outbursts of violence is one of Witkiewicz' basic techniques, heightened here by the cinematographic acceleration.

The Crazy Locomotive is a multisensory spectacle that holds its own against the cinema. Frightful blasts on whistles, the clanking of the cars, the flashing lights, the irrational emotions and wild philosophizing: we are bathed in a free play of vivid sense impressions, accompanying the pursuit of a superreality. Steam from the cylinder cocks obscures the stage; only voices and the rattle of the wheels can be heard. The stage ceases to be a stage in the traditional sense and becomes a playground of sound and color, confused and impenetrable as the higher reality which is sought by Tréfaldi and Travaillac but always eludes them.

The Crazy Locomotive

A PLAY WITHOUT A THESIS
IN TWO ACTS AND AN EPILOGUE

Motto:
"No more rum"
Billy Buns in *Treasure Island* RLS.

From the Commandments for
Locomotive Engineers:
"VI. Women should keep away
from engines; never take them
on your locomotive."
In *The Manual for Frantic
Locomotive Engineers*

Dedicated to

Miss Irena Jankowska

Siegfried Tenser	*Locomotive engineer, 35 years old. Long lean, expressive face. His sharply outlined jaw and arched eyebrows clearly indicate strong will power. Dark Vandyke beard, small mustache. Dressed in a dark jacket and long black trousers with red stripes tucked into yellow leather spats. Cap with a visor.*
Nicholas Slobok	*Locomotive fireman, 28 years old. Completely clean-shaven. His face has coarse, strong features, but you cannot help feeling that there is a hidden streak of appalling languor that spoils his looks. Gray jacket. Green trousers, tucked into high yellow boots.*
Sophia Tenser	*The engineer's wife, 28 years old. Brunette, very pretty and demonic. Elegantly dressed.*
Julia Tomasik	*The fireman's fiancée, 18 years old. Blonde, very pretty, but with an animalistic kind of beauty.*
Turbulence Guster	*An elderly gentleman, dressed for traveling.*
Minna, Countess de Barnhelm	*A hysterical, banal young lady, but not without a certain charm characteristic of old families that have been degenerating for centuries. Dressed for traveling.*
Three Third-Class Passengers	*Look like thugs. One of them is a thief in handcuffs. He claims to be a locomotive engineer.*
Two Gendarmes	*Part of the police escort for the thug in handcuffs. Fantastic uniforms.*
Miss Mira Bean	Dame de compagnie *to Minna—45 years old. Fat, wears glasses.*
Conductor	*In an Austrian uniform, orange piping. A cap.*
Doctor Marcellus Riftmaker	*Young man with dark hair, pointed beard. White uniform. He knows his business.*
Valery Bean	*Mira's brother—fair-haired young man, 30 years old. A bank employee and, in his spare time, a surrealist painter.*

John Cackleson	*Railway guard—reddish beard. Red-green lantern.*
His wife, the beautiful Jeanne Cackleson	*A blonde. Village fortuneteller.*
A crowd of passengers	*They all speak loudly and very distinctly.*

ACT I

The stage represents the back of the locomotive and the front of the tender. The point at which they are attached is a little to the right of the center of the stage. The locomotive can be gigantic—a model which hasn't yet been invented. The train moves to the right. In addition to directions about the right or the left side of the stage, the right and left side of the engine will be indicated according to the direction in which the train is moving. The throttle is of course on the right side. The inside of the engine is brightly lighted by two lanterns. Rods, pipes, and levers, connected with the driving mechanism, are visible, shining by the light of the lanterns. The firebox is open; light streams out of it, and fiery, blood-red flames shoot forth. The locomotive should be constructed in such a way that the empty space between the coal on the tender and the boiler is fairly large (the size of an average room) and that the roof of the locomotive does not cut off the scene of action from the view of those in the balcony. From time to time steam shoots out from the front taps and covers everything. The railroad passageway should be almost two feet high and enclosed by a railway gate, which separates the engine from the rest of the stage.

A person standing on the ground by the locomotive should be visible from the waist up. The scenery at the back of the stage should be produced by means of a movie projector which throws pictures on a screen; the projector will be placed behind the locomotive. At the beginning of the play the background scenery is motionless and represents the station. As the train begins to move, the scenery begins to move to the left (the view from the train in motion). The same sequence of pictures may be repeated occasionally. To go back: at the beginning of the play the scenery represents the railroad station, seen from the platform. The sunset is dying out on the horizon; to the left we see the engine house with its light signals and the silhouettes of locomotives. Semaphores with red and green lights, the arms raised.

Act I begins on an empty platform beyond the station buildings. In the distance, behind the semaphore, we can see the lights of the city whose glow competes with the final light of the sunset. Against this background we see the silhouettes of houses with lights here and there, towers, skyscrapers, clouds, and so on. The firebox which heats the boiler is open. Flames shoot out. The fireman Slobok is filling the firebox by throwing in large chunks of coal as he whistles "The Ideal Tango." This lull does not last long, since Julia soon appears from the left. She is elaborately, but tastelessly dressed. She is carrying a small basket. All the time the train remains standing, the normal noises of a

railroad station can be heard: locomotives whistling, the clank of rail-
road cars being coupled, bells ringing, and the buzz of the crowd.

JULIA Nicholas, I've brought you something to eat. You look as if you're about to explode. Here are some of those little plum cakes you like so much and a bottle of chartreuse.

NICHOLAS (*throws down his shovel and shuts the firebox; the engine begins to snort*) Thanks, Julie. (*He climbs down from the cab, picks up the basket, climbs back up again, leaves the basket in the tender, and climbs down again. He does all this with apelike agility.*)

JULIA (*while Nicholas is climbing up and down*) Where's Mr. Tenser?

NICHOLAS He and his wife have gone to the station for a beer. But you didn't come here to see him.

JULIA And what if I did? What would you know about it, you poor fool? Just look at you, you're covered with coal from head to foot.

NICHOLAS (*having come down again*) Just don't go too far, or I'll really get mad. (*Tenser and his wife approach slowly from the left; his wife is simply yet tastefully dressed. She is carrying a basket.*)

JULIA Do whatever you want. I'm not stopping you. You're always threatening to kill me, anyway.

NICHOLAS Oh . . . if I could only explain it all to you, everything would be different.

JULIA Tell me, then! I'm not afraid.

NICHOLAS (*angrily, in an undertone*) Be quiet. The Tensers are coming.

TENSER What's the steam pressure, Nicholas?

NICHOLAS Six and a half atmospheres, Mr. Tenser.

TENSER Stoke up the fire. (*Nicholas climbs up into the locomotive; feeds the fire; flames shoot out.*) Today I have a feeling I'll need enough steam for six compounds. Once it gains momentum, this beast races along at a frantic clip, but lacks pulling power. And they've gone ahead and attached a sleeping car. (*In a different tone of voice*) Julia, you look very attractive today—perfectly diabolical! But not just diabolical, nor just blonde, but diablondical. Oh . . . if it weren't for this locomotive of mine, everything would be different! It holds me back. Otherwise, I'd just blow up like a hand grenade. (*Sophia tugs at his sleeve.*) Let me alone . . .

JULIA Mr. Tenser always says such . . .

SOPHIA Yes, he's always making up some kind of nonsense. But he's really gentle as a lamb. I can't stand such docile men.

JULIA You must be joking.

SOPHIA I never joke. I was unfaithful to him yesterday with the brakeman on the Nord-Express. And he didn't even bat an eyelash.

JULIA Who? Your husband? Or the brakeman? (*Nicholas slams the firedoor with a bang and leans out of the locomotive cab.*)

TENSER Very funny! Don't pay any attention to them, Nicholas.

NICHOLAS (*angrily*) Sophia, you're corrupting my fiancée. I've asked you not to talk that way in front of her.

JULIA Don't be stupid, Nicholas. I've already been corrupted. I'm well taken care of in that department.

NICHOLAS (*about to climb down from the locomotive*) Shut up, you damned lovebird, or I'll . . . (*His words are interrupted by a toot on the horn which the conductor blows as he appears from the left to signal "All aboard."*)

TENSER We're off! (*He kisses his wife, jumps up into the locomotive, letting out a wild cry which turns into caterwauling. The women run off to the left, Nicholas leans out of the cab.*) Turn on the steam injector! Hurry up! Seven degrees on the water gauge, and . . . (*His words are drowned out by the sound of the train whistle which he has just released. Then he opens the throttle. Steam pours out of the cylinder cocks and obscures the entire stage. When the steam clears away, the landscape has started to move to the left. The wheels can be heard pounding along the tracks, and the locomotive chugs more and more loudly. The last lights of the station disappear. Then the suburbs rush by, and the outskirts of the city are lit by moonlight. A pause.*)

NICHOLAS (*looking at the pressure gauge*) Seven atmospheres. I don't think the valve will stand the pressure.

TENSER (*at the throttle*) And now let's take off our masks! We're on our desert island again: Robinson Crusoe and his man Friday. We're playing the Robinson game the way we did when we were children. (*At this moment city lights appear, and then fields, forests, valleys, and villages rush by.*)

NICHOLAS Mr. Tenser, we can't go on like this any longer! We've got to have a frank talk and settle things—once and for all. Putting aside other, more important matters, tell me: are you by any chance in love with my fiancée?

TENSER (*pushing the throttle down more vigorously*) My dear Nicholas, first throw some more coal on, and then we'll talk.

NICHOLAS Mr. Tenser—the pipes!! . . .

TENSER What do I care about pipes? (*Nicholas feeds the fire; flames shoot out.*) You see, I'm only an ordinary engineer when I want to be—the same way you're just an ordinary fireman. But it probably comes easier to you than to me. (*When Tenser pushes the throttle down, the gestures he makes are exaggerated and impressive. All the while the locomotive chugs along faster and faster.*)

NICHOLAS That remains to be seen. (*He shuts the firebox.*)

TENSER What you're saying is interesting, but right now that's not really the question. Ever since we got on the locomotive, everything's been going well. Except for the minor problem of the next station, we're alone on this iron beast, totally isolated from the rest of the world. We're not only rushing through space, we're intensely aware of it. As Lénart said, there's simply no such thing as relativity of motion for the locomotive engineer. He knows the landscape isn't moving because it's not the landscape he stokes up and oils, but his own locomotive. And the same thing applies to everything that lives and moves. Even a flea's existence disproves all the laws of physics. And that's why the scientific view of relativity can never correspond to reality!

NICHOLAS Mr. Tenser, either you're digressing, or you're joking.

TENSER Just a moment—let me think this through. If the two of us could only—and yet I'd rather do it entirely on my own—if we could construct a planet or meteor, it would be much more comfortable than breaking our necks along these rails. We know only too well where they'll lead us. A boat would be better, but I can't stand water and all the problems connected with it . . . Unfortunately, piracy's no longer possible these days.

NICHOLAS (*intrigued*) So what you're really after is solid financial gain, obtained not altogether legally?

TENSER Oh, no . . . I didn't realize quite what I was saying. Anyhow, just the two of us couldn't handle a ship—and a boat would be too small—there's no solution.

NICHOLAS (*looking at the pressure gauge*) Eight and a half, Mr. Tenser—isn't that too much?

TENSER It can go up to ten. I'm going to need more and more steam from now on, although I don't know exactly why yet. Ever since this morning a kind of vague plan has been taking shape in my mind. For a few minutes, at least, we've got to break through all normal day-to-day relationships. Then everything will become clear. And suddenly we'll reach a stage we never even dreamed of.

NICHOLAS That's strange—ever since this morning I've been thinking about strange and extraordinary things, too, but I couldn't tell you exactly what they were. As I was firing up this beast (he hits the firebox with his fist), something vague and formless began to stir in my brain. But for me the meaning of our existence ultimately becomes shrouded in inner darkness. Only action, not contemplation, can make it clear to us. But we have so few opportunities to do something really extraordinary—if we rule out what you like to call psychological aberrations, Mr. Tenser.

TENSER That's been my experience, too. You're right: I love Julia, but I love my wife, too, although I consider her more as a partner in my various activities, which I'd rather not talk about right now. To me Julia is the essence of all feminine charm and mystery, in spite of—or perhaps because of, her stupidity. But is any of this really very significant? It's all well and good here, but that's why it probably wouldn't mean so much out there, on relatively firm ground. But here, on this pile of metal, plunging ahead on its reckless course, things seem quite different. How can we carry this point of view of ours over into that other sphere which has grown flabby out of sheer inertia and yet at the same time observe everything from this locomotive hurtling through space? That's the problem!

NICHOLAS You know, I was thinking the very same thing myself, but I didn't have it worked out so clearly. I've read a handbook about Einstein's theory, too. The transformation of coordinates, the relativity of everything—and all that.

TENSER But here the question arises: should we be looking from the engine at the ground, or from the ground at the engine? Because on the ground everything I'm saying right now is bound to appear absurd, it's Pure Form,* that's what the FORMISTS call it—I recently read an article on the subject by one of their best essayists. But that's neither here nor there. Let me put it to you quite frankly: say it were possible to transfer life onto this locomotive, how would that be . . . ? Of course the objection could be raised: why not the sleeping car or diner instead? Still, there's a wide gulf between the locomotive and the rest of the train.

NICHOLAS (laughing) Yes, Even I understand the difference. After all, what is life except women, our own and other people's? The eternal rectangle of the husband, wife, and engaged couple, traveling together endlessly on the locomotive? A propos, Mr. Tenser, you know, as soon as we climb aboard this engine-island, I'm not mad at you any more, not even about Julia. Here I'm the fireman, I have my own position in the world. I couldn't put up with any other boss. Everything goes along smoothly here, but it's completely two-dimensional like the surface of a painting—everything stays in its place as if it were frozen, although it's actually moving. Funny, isn't it! (He laughs.)

TENSER Don't make fun of it, Nicholas. It's not so silly as it seems. It's

* A reference to Witkiewicz's own theory of art. [Translators' note]

just that it can't really be done. But what about the idea itself? . . .
Hm . . . (*Pushes the throttle down more vigorously; the engine
chugs faster and faster*) Well, I suppose it could be done, but only
once; it could never be repeated, and it couldn't be done in reverse.
Yes, yes: I think I've got it now—that vague plan of mine.

NICHOLAS But that means death, then.

TENSER (*feverishly*) How do you know?

NICHOLAS Don't touch the throttle. Ninety-two miles an hour,* Mr.
Tenser. Another half mile and we'll reach the point of diminishing
returns. Now's the time to close the throttle.

TENSER Don't try to teach me how to drive this engine. Your job is to
stoke. More coal! Hurry up, Mr. Slobok! (*Nicholas follows the
orders; flames shoot out.*) How do you know my plan means death?
Personally, I don't picture anything as definite as that.

NICHOLAS It's there! (*He points ahead, in the direction the train is
moving.*)

TENSER Perhaps it is there. I like you because of the seismograph you
carry around in your head; you don't even know it's there, but all
the time it's recording obscure tremors on a graph inside you. (*With
admiration*) Such a dumb animal, yet so sensitive to everything. (*A
pause*) More coal. (*Nicholas follows the orders. Flames shoot out.*)

NICHOLAS (*as he's stoking*) So far we're evenly matched. Just think of
it: at the very same moment in history, Existence in all its infinity
and the two of us, alone, on this galloping monster adrift from all
mankind. Even if you tried for a thousand years, you couldn't think
up anything like that.

TENSER What do you mean "adrift from all mankind"? It's true, I
guess. But explain it a little more clearly.

NICHOLAS (*throwing down his shovel*) I already told you: close that
damn throttle and apply the brakes, so Mr. Westinghouse can go
into action, or else we'll probably be derailed at the next curve.
(*Tenser closes the throttle and applies the brakes. The knocking of
the valves on the compressed-air brakes and the clanking of the
wheels can be heard.*)

TENSER Well, go on.

NICHOLAS All you ever think about is women. You'd even like them on
the engine.

TENSER This is the second time you've told me that, Mr. Slobok. To

---

* In accordance with Witkiewicz' remark that the locomotive can be "a model
which hasn't yet been invented," we have increased the speed of the train to
contemporary equivalents by simply turning kilometers per hour into miles per
hour. [Translators' note]

tell the truth, for me a woman is only a symbol: visible proof of the fleeting moment. And what's more I admit I'm a professional seducer. But it's really my way of determining the principal moments of inertia of the body in relation to its axes.*

NICHOLAS But I thought you were somebody more important than that.

TENSER (*trying to distract his attention*) Well, well, well . . . no matter how much nonsense you talk, you still can never be nonsensical enough to get at the Mystery of Existence. Lunatics know that, and so do those on the verge of lunacy.

NICHOLAS Now you're getting off the subject. I'm going to take a chance and tell you the truth: I am not Slobok. Slobok has been lying in his grave for a long time. I'm living his life for him—with the aid of his papers. My name is TRAVAILLAC.

TENSER (*releases the brakes on the engine; the brakes stop clanking*) You've beaten me to it—by half a length. I was just about to introduce myself, too. So you're the great Travaillac, sought in vain by the police all over the world. I could give orders at Dumbell-Junction to have you arrested on the spot.

NICHOLAS (*trying to reach for his back pocket*) I didn't think that you . . .

TENSER Let go of that revolver, Mr. Travaillac. I was only joking. To a criminal of your stature, I too can make my introductions. I am Prince Karl Tréfaldi. I can also be arrested at any station. (*They shake hands.*)

NICHOLAS-TRAVAILLAC Yes, my intuition has never been wrong. If it had, I'd have rotted away in some prison a long time ago. It's a great pleasure for me to make the acquaintance of such a high-class colleague. You were always an inspiration to me in my work. Who knows, perhaps the two of us together can now rise above the turbulent pulp of international depravity.

TENSER-TRÉFALDI Yes—all those crimes bore me, and especially their consequences. Of course I'm not talking about prison, but about inner consequences. Nowadays crime stunts the growth of the human personality. Despite my seeming simplicity, I'm much too complicated to try to lead a normal life. And now there's Julie . . . Oh, don't be offended. Listen to me, Travaillac: we can't go on like this. We've got to do something really diabolical, not to others, but to ourselves, today, right now, without further delay. To put it bluntly, I'm in love with your fiancée, but without a really atrocious

---

* Tenser is evidently a mathematical Don Juan. In physics and engineering, "moment" is a term designating the product of a quantity and a distance to some point associated with the quantity. [Translators' note]

accident, I can't seem to get started. Here, on this engine, at least I'm racing ahead, and that calms me down a little. My wife uses blackmail to keep a hold on me.

TRAVAILLAC What? You mean Erna Abracadabra, the famous chanteuse from Beastly-Hole, New York? The partner of all your crimes?

TRÉFALDI Yes, the very same: she's the one who helped me murder my aunt, the Princess di Boscotrecase. She's dyed her hair black and wears a putty nose. I no longer find her attractive. And that's why I'm still alive today. As for me, I hardly even resemble myself . . .

TRAVAILLAC Of course, we all have to keep changing constantly. But just think: here we are talking about all this, and back there, in one of the cars on the train, someone's reading about the very same thing, a story just like ours, in a murder mystery from the lending library. Funny, isn't it!

TRÉFALDI It's possible; but such a coincidence doesn't diminish either the greatness of our thoughts or the strangeness of our meeting. And now let's get down to business: now I understand what the trouble was! It's what's been torturing me for the last three months. Ever since you became my fireman.

TRAVAILLAC You can be quite frank with me, Karl! I'm prepared for whatever happens!

TRÉFALDI We've got to take some kind of action tonight. Here we are, racing ahead nonstop at breakneck speed, and it's up to us to see it through.

TRAVAILLAC Something like a duel or God's Judgment. Good, that suits my purpose. So you're very much in love with her, in spite of your age, my dear Karl?

TRÉFALDI Yes, but it's a perfectly normal attraction—you understand —I'm not trying to lure her away from you simply because you're a subordinate in one profession and a colleague in another, higher one. We've got to settle the question in a manner befitting outmoded men who have strayed into another epoch and are hopelessly lost.

TRAVAILLAC The aristocracy never has appealed to me. I'm no snob.

TRÉFALDI That doesn't matter: two hundred years ago you certainly would have been a formidable skunk on the summits of humanity. And that's why I'm pushing the throttle down.

TRAVAILLAC All right, but what about the train? The lives of all those people?

TRÉFALDI That from you! A man, or rather a beast, on whose conscience there are at least thirty absolutely monstrous, or rather absolutely glorious murders!

TRAVAILLAC Yes, that's true—but then, in those days I had certain real goals.

TRÉFALDI And isn't our goal tonight much more real than all the other goals we've ever had? We're going to solve the essential problem: the problem of how to make sense out of the whole unsavory comedy of our existence, since our criminal period unfortunately played itself out.

TRAVAILLAC I still haven't been able to grasp the full significance of what we're planning to do—but in principle I'm satisfied with it, I know that. I've simply got to carry it out, because there's nothing else in the world which could possibly give my life any meaning.

TRÉFALDI Don't give it too much thought. Something had to happen. All the territories of crime have already been worked to death. We can't go back to our former lives. And just think how satisfying it will all be if one of us lives through this episode. The survivor will be able to burden the dead corpse with all his guilt—and feel absolutely secure.

TRAVAILLAC All right, I agree. If we pass through Dumbell-Junction without an accident, we're sure to meet No. 50; according to the timetable our paths are bound to cross. There's nothing between stations to stop the other train. I'm prepared for whatever happens, but if both of us survive, it'll be a rather awkward situation.

TRÉFALDI (*opens the throttle wide; the engine begins to snort ferociously*) I hadn't thought about the possibility of being maimed, but now it's too late for such speculation. I'm letting the engine go full steam ahead. (*They shake hands. Julia creeps along the tender by the coal pile.*)

JULIA (*gets up, staggers because the platform between the tender and the locomotive is shaking; the engine chugs faster and faster, and the landscape rushes by madly*) I planned a little surprise for you. You didn't expect it, did you? Mrs. Tenser is coming along on all fours behind me. We jumped on at the last minute. It was difficult crossing over the buffers. Why are you going so fast? It's crazy! There's a station just a little way ahead.

TRAVAILLAC You'll find out soon enough. We'll see whether you're up to the high stakes we're playing for.

JULIA High stakes? What sort of nonsense is that? Have you already drunk up all that chartreuse I gave you? You'll have to hide us till we get to the station—under the coal or somewhere.

TRÉFALDI It's happening: our dreams have come true. We've got to tell them the truth. (*Sophia Tenser, recte * Erna Abracadabra, creeps along the tender.*) Erna, listen to me: I love Julia. Travaillac and I are carrying out God's Judgment. I'm letting the engine rush on, full

---

* Latin, "rightly," to indicate Sophia's real name. [Translators' note]

steam ahead, at breakneck speed. If we come out of this alive—fine; if we're all ground into mincemeat—so much the better. I can't go on any longer constantly threatened by this blackmail. I have a feeling you'll die soon, and you're the only person my conscience wouldn't let me kill. You see—I love you in my own way—you've been a good partner and a good friend. But I think you're destined to die in an accident. You came here of your own free will. It's not my fault. (*The women listen, completely bewildered.*)

ABRACADABRA Who's Travaillac, Siegfried? Have you gone mad? You're suffering from hallucinations.

TRÉFALDI (*pointing to Travaillac*) It's Travaillac, not Slobok. The famous Travaillac. Take a good look at him. Don't you remember? We read about him in *Bulldog Magazine*. All masks are off.

ABRACADABRA Oh, my God! He's gone mad! Mr. Slobok, he's got to be put away! Oh, why did I ever let myself be talked into doing such a ridiculous thing! It's your fault, you snake! (*Throws herself on Julia*) You're the one who persuaded me to jump on the train! (*Travaillac holds Erna back.*)

JULIA Really, I didn't plan it, I didn't know anything about any of this! (*To the men*) But here I am—we're together! And I couldn't be happier! Now I know I love you both. But Mr. Tenser, what a pity that you're not a criminal too, like Nicholas.

ABRACADABRA He's even worse. (*To Travaillac*) Let go of me, you ape! Karl, save me! Close the throttle! I still have a lot to live for!

TRÉFALDI (*cuts the whistle cord in two different places*) Here, Travaillac, tie her up! That's the first time in her life she's ever forgotten her manners. (*He throws Travaillac the cord.*)

JULIE I'll help you. (*They tie up the shrieking Erna.*)

ABRACADABRA Close the throttle! Put on the brakes! I still have a great deal to live for! I've had enough of your dirty, rotten tricks! (*Travaillac gags her and throws her on the coal pile.*)

TRÉFALDI (*to Julia*) To settle the question of whether or not I'm a criminal, may I take the liberty of introducing myself: I am Karl, Prince Tréfaldi—that's quite enough, isn't it?

JULIA No . . . it's you . . . That's incredible! Tréfaldi, the most notorious criminal in the world! Oh—how perfectly marvelous! I'm so happy! I've always dreamed of something really extraordinary happening to me, like in the movies!

TRAVAILLAC Don't I count for something? And don't my crimes mean anything to you? You'd better be careful, Julia; I can kill His Highness and stop the train at any moment.

JULIA (*kissing Travaillac*) I love you both. Now I'm really in love for the first time, and with both of you. At this very moment both of you are extraordinary. Something's being created right here and now, the way it was in the beginning before the world began.

TRÉFALDI Here's a girl who's really worthy of us! We couldn't possibly abandon our plan, could we? We have to do it, Travaillac! We couldn't go on living unless we did it. Isn't that so?

TRAVAILLAC Of course it is! (*Leans out the other side of the engine*) You can already see the signals at Dumbell-Junction.

TRÉFALDI (*looking at the instruments*) Eight and a half atmospheres, 122 miles an hour. I have a feeling we're going to pass right by the station without an accident. I can just see the expression on the faces of all those imbeciles waiting for the train!

ABRACADABRA (*howling through the gag*) Ahrrmbunglohramkopr . . .

JULIA (*clasping her hands together rapturously*) Oh—it's wonderful! It's stupendous! To be with two famous criminals seconds before the crash! I love them both, and they both love me! Oh, this is really living! I'm so excited I could burst! I just can't wait till it happens! (*A frightful blast on the engine whistle interrupts her.*)

ACT II

The same setting as in Act I. The landscape rushes by incredibly fast. During the intermission the film has been changed; a lighted village should flash by for a moment, and then a railroad station with all its lights. On the right side of the engine, Tréfaldi, hanging on to the throttle and leaning out to the right. Everything is bathed in the steam coming out of the cylinder cocks.

TRÉFALDI If we have anything more to say to one another, we'd better say it quickly. In less than a minute we'll pass the first semaphore at Dumbell-Junction. We're going so fast I don't know whether we'll get past the first crossing without being derailed.

TRAVAILLAC What more is there to be said? Eleven atmospheres, 130 miles an hour. My head is hurtling into the infinite cosmic abyss, like a bullet along its trajectory.

JULIA Well, I say I feel marvelous! I've never done anything so exciting before in my whole life, and I'm supposed to be such a hysterical woman. I'd be willing to die a thousand times for a moment like this!

TRÉFALDI As for me, I've nothing more to say. I have the feeling that all my thoughts have been snuffed out of my brain. I'm only an extension of this throttle, as if my brains had been skewered and spitted on this iron lever. But it's more than that; I've become the engine. I'm the one that's racing through space like a bull, ready to impale myself on the blade of my destiny. Yes, it's really a momentous occasion. They ought to put a sign up over our heads: "Do not touch, danger, high voltage!" If a normal person, standing on firm ground, touched me, he'd fall down dead as though struck by lightning. Is this the beginning of mechanized madness?

TRAVAILLAC I'm amazed at your modesty, Karl: first you tell us you have nothing to say, then you talk your head off.

TRÉFALDI But all my talk is negative; I don't have anything positive to say. I only exist as a moving image projected on a screen in the endless void. I think if the engine stopped suddenly, I'd die.

JULIA Oh—stop psychoanalyzing yourself! Real men are always like that, unfortunately, even supermen like you. This is the only time in our lives when we can really gorge ourselves with reality. In our everyday lives we only get scraps, crumbs, and leftovers—that's all there is. But now I have everything—I'm not waiting for anything any more—because I already have it! Even a head-on collision means nothing at all to me. I've got both of you inside the kernel of death that's in me, in you, and in this crazy engine. But in that other life could I ever have had you in some ordinary room, at some ordinary hour of an ordinary night?

ABRACADABRA (*frees herself with a superhuman effort, pulls off the gag, and screams*) I see through you! You filthy slut! I know perfectly well what you want, you rotten little guttersnipe, you gluttonous hunk of vulgar horseflesh! Karl! I appeal to you for the last time! (*Travaillac holds her. They struggle. Julia bursts out laughing—a wild, crazy laugh.*)

TRÉFALDI (*in a thundering voice*) We're coming to the station! I can't let go of the throttle. Throw that trash out—it's got no soul! We're not going to let that disgusting old bag spoil these precious moments with her filthy talk! (*Travaillac and Julia throw Erna Abracadabra out from the left side.*)

TRAVAILLAC (*leans out to see if everything went successfully*) She's smashed to pieces against a pump! Here's the station! The first semaphore! The road is clear! All the crossings are clear. The second semaphore is signaling that the line is occupied. That means No. 50 is on its way to Dumbell-Junction. The crucial moment's drawing near!

TRÉFALDI (*pushes the throttle down; they all dash to the left side of the engine and lean out*) Everything's going well. If only my head didn't feel so insanely empty, I'd really be happy. (*A semaphore rushes by, then the station and its lights; the pounding of the wheels at the crossings can be heard. The crowd on the platform hoots and lets out wild cries. Another semaphore rushes by, then several fac-*

tory chimneys against a background of city lights, and the moonlit landscape starts moving again.)

TRAVAILLAC (*leans out from the left; Julia, from the center; Tréfaldi, from the right*) Someone just jumped onto the moving train! He must be crazy! He'll ruin everything . . .

JULIA (*kissing them rapturously*) Who could possibly be as crazy as we are? We're in a class by ourselves. We're absolutely unique, we're colossal. At last I understand what true greatness is! How grateful I am to you! How I love you both!

TRÉFALDI If No. 50's late, it could mean real trouble. How can we stand this suspense any longer? If our present mood deserts us, there's no guaranteeing what turn the disaster may take.

JULIA Don't talk that way. I could go on like this for hours. A whole lifetime is condensed into these moments of waiting, like a balloon filled with compressed air.

TRAVAILLAC Well, yes, women are generally hardier than men. We can take just so much and no more. If this business drags on, it won't turn out so well; in fact, it could turn out quite badly.

TRÉFALDI Look: someone's crawling along the tender toward us! (*They all look in that direction.*)

A VOICE (*coming from the part of the tender that cannot be seen*) Here they are! Up here! I told you not to give up hope! Something must have happened to the brakes. Come on! We'll help them!

TRAVAILLAC (*trying to reach for his back pocket*) Oh, hell! Now our work is cut out for us! To shoot or not to shoot—I'm not anxious to commit any more crimes! (*In despair*) Oho!—there's a whole gang crawling up here!

TRÉFALDI Don't shoot—it'll all come out all right.

JULIA Nicholas, he's backing down! He's leaving it all up to fate.

TRÉFALDI Look, I'm still doing 115 an hour, and you're complaining. Oh, you're insatiable!

(*Valery Bean, dressed in a cutaway, crawls from the tender over the hunks of coal toward the locomotive. His head is bleeding and bandaged with a bloody handkerchief. His hands are bleeding.*)

BEAN I'm Valery Bean. There's a woman here? What in God's name are you doing here? But what difference does it make? What can I do to help? Tell me quickly, because No. 50 has already left the last station; it's rushing toward us from the opposite direction. Nothing can stop it. The guard's telephone on line No. 20 is out of order. They were talking about it at the station.

JULIA (*in despair*) Nothing beautiful can exist in this world! The human animal always interferes and spoils everything!

TRÉFALDI So it's don't give up hope, is it? Damn! *Sangue del cane!* I'd forgotten about that telephone, and I work for the railroad! Ha, ha ... We'd always counted on speed saving us. That imbecile on the freight train would never be able to back up at 130 miles an hour.

BEAN What are you talking about? She's the lunatic! Have you gone crazy, too? Can't you stop the engine? Tell me what has to be done, and I'll do it. Hurry up!

(*Minna de Barnhelm, her* dame de compagnie, *Mira Bean, Turbulence Guster, three Thugs, and two Gendarmes creep along slowly over the hunks of coal and appear on the locomotive. They are all terrified.*)

TRAVAILLAC You've come at the right time. We need two levers to stop the train: one for me and one for my boss. The throttle's jammed. Lend us your rifles. (*The Gendarmes, frightened to death, hand over their rifles.*) Wonderful! Now beat it! (*Throws the rifles out of the train, to the left, and pulls a revolver out of his pocket*) The situation's getting more and more complicated, but we'll manage somehow. Don't move, or I'll blow your brains out!

BEAN Yes—they really are lunatics! This madness is contagious, it's becoming universal! Unless somebody does something, we're lost. I can't do anything more. I'm worn out from catching the train. I'm completely bushed.

MINNA Isn't there anyone who has enough courage to go after those murderers? In five seconds it may be too late! We'll be killed anyhow, unless someone comes to our rescue! (*Tréfaldi stands with his arms crossed. Next to him Julia, shielded by Travaillac's revolver*)

MIRA BEAN I beg and beseech you! My brother, Valery Bean, is only a bank clerk—it's true he has the reputation of being mad because at night he paints surrealistic paintings, but in spite of that he jumped on a moving train to save me, and he'll save all of us while he's at it. One hundred miles an hour—he was waiting for me at the station with a bouquet of flowers! Can you understand what that means? I was the first one in our car to pull the alarm!

GUSTER Yes, but not one of us has a gun! How could anyone have foreseen this? Such a respectable company! And now we're getting closer and closer to death every second! Death on all sides—it's enough to drive you out of your mind! (*The Conductor appears carrying a lantern.*)

CONDUCTOR Oh, my God, Mr. Guster, what's going on on this train? Nobody has any idea what's happening. The passengers think the train was supposed to pass right by the station. In the rear cars no one had tickets to Dumbell-Junction. Those two have both gone mad. And it's all due to drinking! And I don't have a gun, either!

GUSTER For God's sake, Conductor, let's not waste time arguing! We're not at the theater watching a play! You've got to help us somehow. After all, I know you personally.

CONDUCTOR I don't have any idea what to do. I don't even know where the steering wheel is! All I can do is punch tickets or check whether they've already been punched. Specialization is the great curse of our age. Wouldn't you agree?

THIRD THUG (*in handcuffs*) Mr. Guster, we're personally acquainted, too, but in a rather odd sort of way. I attacked you on the street one night, even though we've never been formally introduced. Please accept my apologies and see about getting these handcuffs taken off. I used to be an engineer.

GUSTER (*to the Gendarmes*) Take his handcuffs off.

MINNA (*to the Third Thug*) Save us, and I'll have you released from prison. My uncle is prosecutor in the appellate court. I fell in love with the fireman two minutes ago. He's my type. I've found him at last. I've got to get him away from that girl so we can live together for the rest of our lives—without any interference! I want to live! Don't you understand: Fireman, did you hear that? (*The three lunatics burst out laughing, diabolically. Meanwhile the Gendarmes unlock the handcuffs on the Third Thug.*)

TRAVAILLAC You know, that girl's a real addition to our group. It makes the situation more varied.

TRÉFALDI Seven separate destinies fatally meet at one point—it's almost mathematically inevitable. There's nothing more to be said on that subject—except the clichés second-rate dramatists use to pad out their vacuous plays. We'll just wait and see. Right now I wonder if I'll have enough courage. Julie, if we're saved, you won't be false to us, will you?

JULIA Never! I'm a superwoman, from another world. But it makes me furious they've ruined such a wonderful experience for us!

MINNA You disgusting phony! Now I see what tricks you've used to hold onto your handsome fireman!

TRAVAILLAC Karl, come here by the throttle, just in case! They're so desperate they're capable of anything!

CONDUCTOR (*holding up his lantern*) Karl? He's been Siegfried all his life!

TRÉFALDI (*edging along the boiler to the right-hand side of the engine*) Not all of it, my friend! If you live through this, there'll be even more surprises! You know, Travaillac, perhaps it's all to the good that they've come up here! It gives me the strength to go on. If it weren't for this, I admit I might have backed down in the face of death. So it's best after all to leave some odds and ends to the miserable workings of chance.

JULIA I admire your heroism in admitting your shortcomings, Karl.

GUSTER It's shocking that at this stage of civilization our lives are in the hands of such people. I just can't believe I'm here on this locomotive! (*Valery Bean faints and falls on the coal pile. All the others are extremely excited as they wait for the results of freeing the Thug.*)

TRAVAILLAC (*to Guster*) And did you think we're all lifeless manikins like you? We criminals are the only people who count for anything in this degraded world, especially those of us who are criminals, not for the sake of money or for any other motive, but for the sake of crime itself.

JULIA Yes—criminals and maybe artists, too! They're the only ones who are really alive. Of course I only know artists through their works. Maybe lunatics are, too? But I don't know any lunatics.

THIRD THUG (*the one who's been released*) Come off it! They're lunatics, aren't they? And what about you? Aren't you a lunatic?

MINNA It's all a hoax, a hideous joke! It's due to the influence of modern art!

THIRD THUG (*set free*) All right now, just hold them to one side, and I'll try to stop the engine. Hurry up, there's something whistling up there ahead of us. (*Guster, the other two Thugs and both the Gendarmes push one another forward. No one has the courage.*)

MINNA Ha! Since not one of you has the courage, I'll have to do it myself! Wretched cowards!

THIRD THUG (*his hands in his pockets*) Only the biggest cowards are really brave, and that's because they're afraid; your average coward just can't make it. (*While he is saying this, Minna grabs the shovel and hits Tréfaldi on the head; he falls on the guardrail. Encouraged, the others throw themselves on Travaillac. He fires two shots from his revolver and misses both times. Travaillac is overpowered. The Third Thug closes the throttle again to make reverse steam and says*) The link in the Heisinger von Waldeck system. A beautiful gadget—in my day we didn't have anything like it. (*A violent clang is heard inside the engine. Julia remains leaning against the boiler. She holds her head in her hands. The others utter a cry of joy.*)

GUSTER (*leaning out from the left side of the engine, shouts in despair*): Too late! No. 50's rushing toward us at top speed! We won't be able to stop! Blow the whistle, what's-your-name! Hurry! (*The Third Thug forces a forlorn whistle out of the engine.*

Despairing cries. In a frenzy of fear, all the characters look about wildly and let go of Travaillac.)

TRAVAILLAC (*shouting*): Julia! Don't be afraid! Now you'll be mine! My boss got his belly split wide open, and he's kicked the bucket! He died muttering obscenities.

MINNA No, you're mine! Mine! Mine! We'll die together! There'll be nothing left of us but glue! (*She kisses Travaillac; he tears himself away. Minna's* dame de compagnie *Mira pulls her away from Travaillac. At this very moment a terrible crash and din are heard. Steam covers everything, as the engine bursts into fragments.)*

EPILOGUE

Stationary landscape. Night, moonlight. White clouds are floating across the sky. All that remains of the wrecked engine is a heap of debris. A crowd of passengers. Groans and cries. Railway guard Cackleson, with a red lantern in his hand, is talking to the Conductor. The dead and wounded are being pulled out.

GUARD Conductor, what's happened? Were there a lot of people in the locomotive? Was there a shooting? Was it a holdup?

CONDUCTOR (*holds onto his head; his shako is gone, and his coat is in shreds*): P-po-po-po-po-po-po-po...Oh, Oh...my God, my God...

GUARD Talk like a human being. As soon as I saw what was going on, I immediately gave the signal to stop—for both you and No. 50. You must have gone right by the station, or else my clock isn't running right. My wife's gone mad—she's been delirious all day. And then that telephone that's been out of order since five o'clock! I don't want to be held responsible for this. (*The Conductor spreads his arms, babbles incoherently, then speaks.*)

CONDUCTOR It's-s-s a m-m-mystery!!! It's a miracle that I'm still alive. My brain's like mush, and there's a hole in my head. In a minute it'll all run out through the hole (*They pull Julia out; she runs to the front of the stage screaming.*)

JULIA (*wildly*) Nothing beautiful can exist in life! Everything's rotten! Everything beautiful has come to an end for all time! I've had enough! Kill me! I don't want anything, I don't want to see anything or know anything! I don't know whether I'm really myself or not. I don't know what'll happen next. Meaningless words are strung out through my empty brain. Everything is strange and horrible at the same time; nothing's what it really is; it's all

*I have seen an explosion like this and the collapse of a building in Björnson's play, *Beyond Human Power* (at the Cracow theater). I know that it is feasible from the technical point of view. [Author's note]

horrible at the same time; nothing's what it really is; it's all something else. I'm so afraid! I don't know whether these people are really alive. (*Points to those present*) A black abyss, soft and impersonal, is opening up before me! (*She sits down on a heap of debris.*)

GUARD She's gone out of her mind from nervous shock. She's talking exactly like my wife. (*From under the debris they pull Tréfaldi and also the bodies of the three Thugs and the Second Gendarme.*)

FIRST GENDARME Yes, yes—those three thugs and my buddy are already nothing but a mass of pulp. (*Pointing to Tréfaldi*) That one there—he's the chief culprit. Grab him!

TRÉFALDI Don't you see, my good man, that all my guts are spilling out? I'm almost dead. The throttle went into my belly at least twelve inches. (*They pull out Travaillac and Minna, who are safe and sound.*) Besides, that young lady hit me on the head with a shovel (*he points to Minna*), and I'm still suffering from nervous shock.

MINNA We're safe and sound. Come on, Slobok; forget about that woman and all the horrible things she made you do. You'll completely regain your equilibrium with me.

TRAVAILLAC That's true, but what about my part in what happened? After all, there were witnesses. Not everything went the way it was supposed to. After what I've been through, all I want is peace and quiet.

MINNA That's easy to arrange. You'll spend six months in a lunatic asylum and get a good rest. Then I'll have you released. My uncle is the prosecutor in the appellate court. You've got to live and go free. You're my type. Even though I'm a Countess, I'd never find another man like you. (*To the Gendarme*) I'll take this fireman with me, on my own responsibility. (*The Gendarme salutes.*)

TRAVAILLAC If that's the way it's going to be, there's no point in resisting. Good-bye, Conductor. Unfortunately, it's beginning all over again for me. We have Julia and her influence to thank for all the strange things we've been through. I've had enough hysterical women to last me a lifetime! (*He and Minna go out to the left.*)

GUSTER (*crawling out from under the wreckage*) The Beans were squashed into a jelly and chopped up like cabbage. I'm all splattered with Miss Mira's guts. It seems to me it's all been a dream. (*Jeanne Cackleson enters. Disheveled hair, dressed all in white, decked out in flowers like Ophelia. She calmly observes the scene.*)

CONDUCTOR Let's go have a beer, Cackleson. We'll have time for quite a few before all this gets straightened out. The ambulance train will take care of the rest. I hope this doesn't start an epidemic among engineers throughout the whole world!

JEANNE CACKELSON (*coming up to Julia and hugging her*) I know everything, too, the way whe does. Only the two of us know—all the rest of you are fools. I've always waited. I waited every time a train came by. You can't imagine what torture it is to wait and watch the trains come by and then rush away somewhere, carrying all those passengers off! Then finally I stopped waiting! Today at five o'clock I cut the telephone line. During the night, a spirit told me I had to do it. He had a dark beard, and his eyes gleamed like a cat's. He's the one I was unfaithful to my husband with while I was asleep. Ha, ha, ha!!

GUARD Jeanne, calm down and go back home. It's sickening to have to listen to you talk that way!

TRÉFALDI (*growing excited*) Jeanne! Why didn't I meet you before? I'd certainly have seduced you!

JEANNE He's the one! He's the one I dreamed about during the night! (*She falls to the ground with a wild yell. Julia kisses her. Dr. Marcellus Riftmaker and two Gendarmes run in from the left side.*)

DR. RIFTMAKER (*pointing to Tréfaldi*) First of all, let's save this one! He's the greatest criminal in the whole world, the famous Prince Tréfaldi, king of murderers. At least he's got to live so he can atone for his crimes and be an example to others. (*On his knees by Tréfaldi*) The police received a telegram. We came by handcar from Dumbell-Junction. He was to be arrested there. The public didn't suspect anything. (*Examines Tréfaldi*) Damn!—there's no getting around that! His insides are out!

TRÉFALDI Too late, Doctor! Even to please the court, I can't postpone the hour of my death. I had an inkling of it, but I swear I didn't know anything definite. I die without any regrets, so you can cheer up. Good-bye. (*He dies. They all take off their hats.*)

GUARD Doctor, forget about those murderers and, instead, please look after the women! (*Points to his wife and Julia*) They've both gone completely mad!

DR. RIFTMAKER (*getting up*) Just a minute, just a minute, my good man. Justice first, then the wounded, and the mentally ill last of all, because there's absolutely nothing we can do to thelp them.

CURTAIN

End of the Epilogue and of the Play

CPSIA information can be obtained at www.ICGtesting.com
Printed in the USA
LVOW07s0418010815

448359LV00016B/107/P